MY MOM WANTS THIS, BUT I WANT THAT

High School Planning Guide for Educators, Parents, and Students

Dr. Dedra Lori Muhammad

Rising South Literacy School

Cover design by Hanif Louis Muhammad

Printed in the United States of America

This book is dedicated to stakeholders -administrators, counselors, and teachers who work tirelessly on behalf of our students. This is dedicated to parents and caregivers of middle and high school students concerned about their young scholar's future success. This book is dedicated to students who need essential support navigating through the high school process and tertiary planning.

CONTENTS

FOREWORD

This book is a valuable reference tool for teachers, counselors, administrators, parents, and students. It is a compilation of blogs, resource lists, short stories, essays, emails, and how-to sections— everything needed to aid students in their high school to post-secondary journey. The topics range from advice on planning, timelines, understanding how scholarships work, the truth about letters of recommendation, consideration for student-athletes, types of careers, career interest inventories, resources, post-secondary planning terms every high school student should know, jobs in Engineering and STEM, liberal arts, gap years, graduating early, student-parent scenarios, and so much more! Ask about the workbook that aligns with this guide.

INTRODUCTION

Chandra's Story: I'm Not Going to College if I Can't Play Ball There.

Chandra was an exceptional basketball player, and everyone knew it. At age 13, she had reached 5"10 and had the agility and flexibility of a sleek feline. She stopped playing intramural or club ball in the summer of her seventh-grade year to focus on high school sports, as she had made the varsity team as an eighth grader. She rotated between a power forward and a center player until tenth grade. By her sophomore year, she was being scouted by Division I-level schools nationwide.

With such a bright athletic future, Chandra took the advice of her grandfather, who had played for the University of Michigan in the seventies. She, too, would be a Michigan Wolverine and compete in the Big Ten Conference. Chandra was proud of her uncle's accomplishments. It seemed like everyone in the city either knew him or had heard how good he was as a baller back in his day. Whenever she would go places with him, his friends and other relatives remarked how Chandra was following his footprints.

As a junior, coaches started pressing her. At first, she was only getting letters, but later, they asked to set up phone conferences with her. They wanted to know about her grades and ACT scores and if she was registered with the Clearinghouse. Because of Chandra's score of 15 on the ACT, she found she was not eligible to compete at Division I or II schools. Then, in a miraculous turn of events, the woes of COVID-19 influenced a ruling that meant ACT scores were no longer considered by the NCAA in determining a student's athletic eligibility! However, the admissions office at her three top schools still used the ACT as an admissions criterion. She surely thought the coaching staff at the University of Michigan could make an exception for her, but she was wrong. She was too embarrassed to entertain attending a Division III or junior college (JUCO), even though she desperately wanted to compete.

Chandra could play ball but could not get into the University of Michigan. She found out the coaches could recruit her. Still, they had no authority in the admissions office: To attempt to sway or influence her admissions application based on athletics would be an NCAA Clearinghouse violation.

She did not want to hear about how some of the best athletes start at JUCO. She was Chandra, the one everyone expected so much from. She had to go to a DI school, which had to be one of the best schools in the country.

Chandra felt a tinge of bitterness under her tongue as though she had swallowed a tablespoon of salt mixed with WD-40. How could her grandfather never mention her grades? Sure, he kept at her by repeating she needed to keep her grades up, but he had no idea what her grade point average was, and no one told her to be concerned about the ACT or the PSAT as a sophomore. Furthermore, she did not know a 3.0 would not be enough to land her many (merit) scholarships if she didn't have a corresponding ACT or SAT score. The admissions office did not like the "lack of rigor" demonstrated on her transcript, so Chandra could not land any merit scholarships, whatever those were.

Chandra didn't know much about local scholarships or the dozens of ways to help pay for college. The only type of scholarship she had heard about--and not much about, apparently, were athletic scholarships. Finding this out in her senior year was a nightmare. Her mind raced backward to where she went wrong, what she was supposed to do, and when? When did she miss the memo, and who was responsible for sending it?

Chandra was moderately consoled to learn a few DI schools could still offer her scholarships because they waived their ACT requirement. They were offering her partial scholarships. However, her peers told her to see her college counselor for help. There must be a way Chandra could make the most out of her situation.

For so many students like Chandra and those with vastly different yet equally harrowing situations, it is essential to understand the process and start planning and learning everything about the postsecondary journey as early as possible.

POST-SECONDARY PLANNING TERMS

The glossary below contains words associated with high school experience and culture, graduating from high school, and moving on to the next level.

Advanced Placement (AP Class)

Advanced Placement (AP) classes are college-level classes offered as part of the student's high school curriculum options. Students earn high school credit for passing the class, and they can also earn college credit based on the score earned on the AP exam and the college's requirements. Each college has its guidelines for awarding credit due to AP exams. If a student makes a 3, some colleges accept the score, whereas others require a four on the AP exam to receive credit in an equivalent course.

American College Test (ACT)

The American College Test (ACT) is the most widely known college admittance exam. A perfect score on the ACT is 36. An 18 is considered average. Many public universities accept an 18 on the ACT to mean the student has a 50% chance of success in college. This depends on the rigor of the university/college, of course. Students typically take the ACT in their junior high school year but can take it at any time, given that it is a paid-for test. The cost in 2023 was $66.00. The ACT plus the Writing portion was $91.00. Included in the registration fee, students can send their scores to up to four schools. After Covid-19, many schools became "test-optional" and discontinued requiring the ACT. However, the ACT might still be needed for that same school to qualify for specific scholarships.

Associate Degree

A degree awarded after a student completes a two-year program.

At-Risk

Refers to students or groups with a higher likelihood of academic failure or not completing high school in four years. This can include homelessness, incarceration, teenage pregnancy, serious health issues, domestic violence, migrant-worker families, or other conditions. It can also encompass learning disabilities, low test scores, disciplinary problems, grade retention, or other factors negatively impacting a student's educational performance. Educators may use this term broadly for general populations or specifically for individual students who demonstrate persistent behaviors or circumstances.

Baby Boomers

The oldest teachers in the building. LOL. They are a demographic cohort group of people born between 1946 and 1964.

Bachelor's Degree (B.A., B.S.)

A bachelor's degree is an undergraduate academic degree students can pursue after completing high school or its equivalent. It provides a foundation in a specific field of study and is considered the first higher education level.

Class Rank/GPA Substitution

High-class ranks and grade point averages can be used as a merit for **automatic admission** into some colleges. This is an excellent opportunity for students with low ACT/SAT scores. With Class Rank and GPA substitutions, students may be eligible for the same scholarships at that school as students who submitted test scores. Texas A&M is an example of a school that offers Class Rank/GPA substitution.

CLEP Exams

CLEP exams assess introductory college course material. The College Board has designed CLEP exams to evaluate fundamental college-level subject matter, much like AP exams. By obtaining a passing score on a single CLEP exam, students can earn three or more credits, potentially saving an average of $2,700 on a three-hour college course.

Cohort (Educational)

The term refers to a grade level or class of students who attend school during the same period. Whenever students enter the 8th grade together, that cohort would eventually graduate together.

Common Applications -Common applications are centralized college application platforms. This book lists more information about the Common Application under "**Tools and Resources**" in this book.

The Common Application - The Common Application, often called the Common App, is the most popular centralized college application platform. Hundreds of colleges and universities in the United States and several other countries use it. It is designed to streamline the college application process for students applying to multiple institutions.

Black College Application - There is also the Black College Application with roughly 68 member schools (See the "Tools and Resources" chapter for links and more information).

Coalition Application -and the Coalition Applications with over 150 member schools. (See the "Tools and Resources" chapter for links and more information).

Conditional (or provisional) Acceptance Into College

Conditional or provisional acceptance into college is when a college accepts students based on specific requirements they must fulfill. It means the college considers the student a promising candidate but needs additional information or actions to complete the acceptance and enrollment. The student's next steps and research will depend on the institution's specific conditions. For instance, if one of the conditions is achieving a high score on a standardized test, the student can research how to take the test and find study tips to prepare adequately.

Cooperative Education (Co-Op)

Co-op is short for Cooperative Education, a practice that combines classroom theories with practical, real work applications. Students in Co-op programs usually attend core classes at their high school and have jobs outside of school. The Co-Op instructor meets with these students in a classroom setting and teaches the related curriculum.

C.S.S. Profile (College Scholarship Service Profile)

The CSS Profile is an online application generated by the College Board that allows college students to apply for non-federal financial aid. This application for institutional financial support is required by approximately 300 (usually private) colleges and universities and a sprinkle of scholarship organizations.

Dual Enrollment (DE)

Dual Enrollment (DE) is when a student enrolls simultaneously in two different academic programs or schools. This allows them to take college-level courses while still in high school. To participate in a DE program, the college must have an agreement with the student's school district. To apply, the student must go through their high school and the college. For instance, a student who wants to take collegiate-level courses while still in high school would begin the application process at their high school and earn approval by meeting the Grade Point Average requirement and requisite grade level. Once the high school approves the application, the college typically approves as well. Another version of DE is Early College.

Early Action (College Application)

Early Action means a student would apply much earlier than general applicants during a set period. With EA, even though students would receive an admission decision early, they are not required to commit to that college early. Early Action differs from Early Decision because students must commit in the latter scenario. Students choose EA if they believe they have found the "perfect" college but still want to continue exploring college options and offers.

Early Decision

Early Decision (ED) represents a binding agreement. Students apply very early in the application process, and if they are admitted, they must commit to that school. Early Decision typically comes with higher acceptance odds.

Early Graduation (from High School)

Students who matriculate from high school ahead of their cohort are considered early graduates. Instead of students graduating in May or June, they elect to graduate a semester early in December. Other students choose to graduate at the end of their junior year if they have enough credits. Each school has a procedure students must follow to graduate early.

FAFSA -Free Application for Federal Student Aid

The FAFSA is a form used to apply for federal financial aid for higher education. It is linked to the income tax information of each family in the United States. Nowadays, many public schools require students to complete the FAFSA to graduate. Parents and students should fill out the FAFSA together unless the student is not living with their parents. Completing the FAFSA is the only way for students to be eligible for federal college grants and for consideration for work-study (on-campus jobs) and some scholarships.

FAFSA I.D.: The FAFSA I.D. must be created before one can complete the FAFSA. Parents and students need the FAFSA I.D. to sign the FAFSA. One parent and the student each need to create their own FSA ID.

FERPA – Family Educational Rights and Privacy Act

Students have the right to access their school records, and they have the right to have their records kept private. A student may be asked to waive his FERPA rights to allow someone to write a letter of

3

recommendation (LOR) for said student without the student being privy to the LOR.

Financial Aid

Any aid or money a student would use for college or trade school. Financial aid comes in the form of scholarships, federal grants, student work-study, and loans.

Gap Year

A gap year is typically when students take a break from formal education to engage in other activities, such as traveling, working, volunteering, or pursuing personal interests. There are multiple pros and cons associated with taking a gap year.

Graduate Student

Any student working on a higher degree beyond a bachelor's degree.

HBCU (Historically Black Colleges and Universities)

Historically Black Colleges and Universities (HBCUs) were erected specifically to serve Black students in response to Black students' mass predominantly White institutions (PWIs) disqualification.

Helicopter Parents

A protective type of parenting with pros and cons. The name came about to describe the way some parents hover excessively over their children. They have been described as parents who apply intense pressure to micromanage the affairs of their offspring. Helicopter parents also deliver security, commitment, and dependability; they show interest and are wholly invested in their student's success.

Juris Doctorate

A Juris Doctorate (J.D.) is a professional degree required to become a lawyer in the United States. It is typically pursued after completing a bachelor's degree.

Master's Degree (M.A., MS.)

A master's degree is a postgraduate academic degree pursued after completing a bachelor's degree. It allows students to specialize in a particular field of study or area of professional practice and gain advanced knowledge and skills in that area.

M.D.

An M.D. is a medical doctor. There are many types of medical doctors with specialized areas. For example, a psychiatrist is an M.D. because they prescribe medicine. See the section on Degree Types.

NCAA Clearinghouse

The NCAA Clearinghouse clears a high school student to play Division I or II collegiate athletics. The organization has a set of rules, including a transcript audit to determine eligibility for student-athletes to be able to participate at an NCAA Division I or II college as a student-athlete.

Net Price

The dollar amount a student pays to attend a particular college.

Net Price Calculator

A tool that analyzes the expected financial aid to determine the total cost for a student to attend that school. If a college receives federal funding, they will likely provide a net price calculator on their site. Schools either use a federal template or their calculator.

Ph.D.

Doctor of Philosophy in any field. This is a non-medical degree. The holder of a Ph.D. has done extensive research in their field of study and is considered an expert. An average Ph.D. program is approximately four additional years of study beyond a master's degree.

Portfolio

A compilation of important student work highlighting strengths and gifts. Portfolios can demonstrate student growth and achievements. Students can create an art portfolio or a portfolio with cybersecurity projects; they can include various projects where the student excelled.

Post-secondary

The time and events that occur after high school graduation. Post-secondary planning represents students' activities to prepare for their immediate path following high school.

Rigor

Classes that are more academically challenging are said to have more rigor. When students take Advanced Placement, International Baccalaureate (IB), Dual Enrollment, and other difficult courses, their transcript shows severity. The student's GPA is separate from the strength of the course. As such, a lower grade in a more rigorous course is understandable.

Scholarship

Aid that is earmarked for college and is awarded following a contest or application. Like grants, scholarships do not need to be paid back. Students can apply for scholarships early. Middle school students and ninth graders can apply for scholarships. When scholarships are awarded, they are most likely paid to the financial aid department at the institution of higher learning where the student has committed to attend. Most scholarship applications are online, but several others are physical applications that students must complete and mail.

Standardized Test

When all test takers are required to answer the same questions, it results in consistent scoring. Standardized tests aim to eliminate subjective measuring, which means that when students take standardized tests, their results can be compared fairly. Unlike grades given by teachers, which can be subjective, it cannot be assumed that students with the same grades in different parts of the country have the same level of intelligence. However, with standardized tests, it is generally accepted that the results can be used to compare students' intelligence across different regions. Nevertheless, some argue that standardized tests are not fair measures for certain groups of students based on their cultural background.

Preliminary Scholastic Achievement Test (PSAT)

The PSAT/NMSQT is designed for grades 9-11 but is generally offered to 10th and 11th graders. It assesses the critical reading, mathematics, problem-solving, and writing skills that students have acquired. Taking the PSAT/NMSQT is the ideal way to prepare for the SAT. Juniors take the test to be considered for the National Merit Scholarship Corporation's scholarship programs. This scholarship can only be obtained by taking the PSAT.

Scholastic Achievement Test (SAT)

The SAT is a college admissions exam that differs from the ACT in measuring a student's aptitude for learning. Where the ACT measures achievement based on coursework, the SAT measures future achievement. The SAT evaluates computational ability and reading comprehension. The test detects talents and aptitude, especially among students from underprivileged backgrounds and other diamonds in the rough.

Senioritis

Senioritis is a highly contagious condition that affects students of all ages and academic backgrounds as they approach the end of the school year. It's characterized by an extreme lack of motivation, a sudden fascination with Netflix binges, and a chronic case of "just one more episode" syndrome. Symptoms include a strong desire for freedom, a tendency to daydream about summer vacation, and an uncanny ability to find every excuse to avoid studying or completing assignments.

Test Blind Colleges

Institutions that do not consider standardized test scores (such as the SAT or ACT) as part of their admissions process. This means these colleges make admissions decisions based solely on factors like high school grades, extracurricular activities, essays, letters of recommendation, and interviews without considering standardized test scores. Popular test-optional colleges and universities include the University of Chicago, Wake Forest University, Bowdoin College, Bucknell University, Pitzer College, and Brandeis University.

Test Flexible

Schools that allow students to submit alternative test scores as a part of their admission process. For example, a school may accept an Advanced Placement (AP) score instead of the ACT. Acceptable scores will vary depending on the institution. Still, you can generally fulfill the SAT/ACT requirement by submitting scores from AP exams, IB tests, and school-administered placement tests.

Test-flexible schools used to be more common before the pandemic, but now many schools have switched to a test-optional policy. NYU is the only well-known test-flexible school (and they are currently test-optional due to the pandemic).

Transcripts and Final Transcripts

A transcript summarizes credit-bearing grades that students accumulate during their entire high school tenure, including any middle school grades that a school district will honor credit for, such as Algebra 1. Every junior and senior needs to know the procedure at their high school for ordering their transcript. A final transcript can usually be requested about two weeks after students graduate high school.

Undergraduate

Students enrolled or enrolling in college who have not yet earned a four-year degree. High school students who enter college for the first time are called undergraduates.

CHAPTER 1: STUDENTS, YOU ARE THE ULTIMATE COMMODITY!

Students, you are the shining stars and the valuable assets everyone desires. You are not just a tiny part of a large group. When my students get accepted into college, they express great excitement, and I remind them of how fortunate the college is to have them. You are investing thousands of dollars into your education and can choose from various schools. Your talents, community service, unique qualities, and charming personalities add liveliness to college campuses and industries. Companies are also seeking high school graduates, offering competitive salaries. As a college and career counselor, I can attest to the high demand for students like you.

Have you considered the impact of COVID-19 on the attendance of companies, colleges, and universities? Each state has a target number of qualified workers who should enter the workforce straight out of high school to maintain the economy in that region. Schools rely on a sufficient number of first-year students to fill vacancies, and you are the sought-after resource.

It's crucial to remember that attending a public institution can be a significant financial investment, even with scholarships. Some students may feel that the university is doing them a favor by accepting their tuition fees, but it's important to recognize your worth and have confidence in yourself.

Your Uniqueness: Environments may have an impact, but let me tell you, your burning desire to be the best outweighs any obstacle that comes your way. We've seen students from all walks of life rise above their circumstances and achieve greatness. I won't sugarcoat it; life isn't always fair and square, but guess what? You are the wild card, the game-changer who can drive the final result. Your determination, resilience, and inner fire make you a force to be reckoned with.

You Are the Commodity: It's time to unleash your inner superstar. Being a commodity means you're a valuable product, a rare gem in mediocrity. You bring something special, something that sets you apart from the average student...unless it is you who chooses to be moderate. If you accept your greatness, you're like the VIP pass that workforce developers and admission/scholarship committees can't resist. Your qualities and characteristics add immense value, making you a standout candidate among your competitors. Just like a highly sought-after product, your worth increases based on demand. So, take a moment to appreciate your awesomeness because you're in high need!

The Excitement of Acceptance: Picture this, my friends: You receive that acceptance letter, and your heart dances happily. It's pure exhilaration, a new chapter waiting to unfold. But here's the thing: That excitement isn't a one-sided affair. Oh no, you must understand your worth in this equation. You were chosen. After all, you meet the requirements because you're a stellar student capable of representing the university with flying colors. They want you as much as you want them. You bring something unique to the table, and the college knows it. So, bask in that excitement and let it fuel your confidence.

Increasing Your Worth: Here's a pro tip for further boosting your value: Get involved, my friends! Join clubs, organizations, and activities that light up your passion. Show the college administrators that you're academically remarkable and a social powerhouse. Your involvement adds to the campus community, creating a vibrant atmosphere that keeps students engaged and less likely to drop out. So, put on your superhero cape and become a campus superstar!

Conditional Acceptance and Appeals: Now, for those of you who might have been accepted conditionally or had to go through the appeal process, understand that the bottom line is that schools need to ensure their students can graduate promptly. But fear not, my fabulous bunch, because you can shine bright. Consider where you can be an asset to the university and where you can showcase your talents and skills. Choose a school that aligns with your goals rather than being swayed solely by glamor. It's all about finding the perfect match where you can be the star that you are.

Always remember this: You are not just a number or a statistic. You are the ultimate commodity, the one everyone wants to snatch up. Embrace your awesomeness and show the world what you're made of. Remember, you are the star of your story, and there's no limit to what you can achieve. So go out there, rock those acceptance letters, and let your wit, humor, and incredible potential shine brightly. You've got this, and the world better be ready for the unstoppable force that is you!

Choosing Your Path

First things first: It's perfectly okay if you don't know your career path. Remember, you can explore and change your mind along the way. Everyone will not have a career path. For example, some young ladies marry right after high school, start immediately as homemakers and mothers, and never enter the workforce or college. That is still a path.

You need to figure out whether your intended career requires schooling beyond high school as early as possible. If so, learn early what the requirements are for getting into the school of your choice. Choose your dream school, a middle ground school you can live with, and choose a school that may not be at the top of your list but one that might be the most practical option.

Now, let's talk about the importance of considering your financial future. While it's true that pursuing a career you love is crucial, it's also essential to be realistic about the financial aspects. Corporate jobs, for instance, may not always provide the stability we hope for, with companies folding and unexpected layoffs. That's why developing a skill set that can empower you to be self-sufficient is crucial. Ask yourself: What can you do to make money independently? What's your backup plan or sidekick job? Multiple income streams are valuable, and learning how to manage and grow your money is equally important.

If you're considering a liberal arts degree, it's wise to research in advance how much careers in that field typically pay. For instance, with a bachelor's degree in psychology, you might find that pursuing higher education, such as a master's or doctoral degree, could significantly impact your earning potential. Understanding the financial implications of your chosen field will help you make informed decisions. What job do you think you can get with a B.A. in Psychology? Would such a stand-alone degree be worth the investment of earning the degree? How long will it take you to see a return on your investment?

Lastly, flexibility is critical. Your interests and goals may evolve, and that's perfectly normal. By staying open-minded, you can adapt to new opportunities and discover unexpected paths that align with your passions and financial aspirations. Remember, balancing choosing a career you enjoy and considering the economic prospects is essential. Both factors play a significant role in shaping your future. So, as you embark on this exciting journey, explore, gather information, be open to new possibilities, and make informed decisions that align with your interests, passion, and long-term financial goals.

Of Course, Money Matters

Understanding the importance of money is crucial for students as they navigate their financial future. Students must grasp the significance of money management and investing.

Financial Security: Money provides financial security, allowing individuals to cover their basic needs, handle unexpected expenses, and build a safety net for emergencies. Having enough savings for a rainy day helps protect against financial hardship during unforeseen circumstances like medical emergencies, job loss, or significant repairs.

Retirement Planning: Saving and investing money for retirement is essential. Students should start saving early, take advantage of retirement accounts like 401(k) or Individual Retirement Accounts (IRAs), and contribute consistently over time. By doing so, they can harness the power of compounding interest and potentially grow their investments significantly, providing a comfortable retirement lifestyle.

Financial Freedom and Independence: Learning to manage money effectively can lead to financial freedom. It allows individuals to control their life choices, pursue their passions, and make decisions based on personal fulfillment rather than financial constraints. Individuals can achieve financial independence by saving and investing wisely, which means having enough assets to generate income to cover their expenses without relying solely on a job.

Multiple Streams of Income: Students must understand the importance of diversifying their income sources. Relying solely on one job may limit their financial opportunities and increase their vulnerability to economic uncertainties. Students should explore various avenues for generating income, such as part-time jobs, freelance work, starting a small business, social media platforms, or investing in income-generating assets like rental properties or dividend-paying stocks.

Money Management and Budgeting: Learning how to budget and manage money is fundamental. Students should practice tracking expenses, distinguishing between needs and wants, setting financial goals, and creating a realistic budget. This helps them prioritize spending, avoid unnecessary debt, and make informed financial decisions.

The Power of Investments: Investing is a way to grow money over time. By allocating money into different investment vehicles like stocks, bonds, mutual funds, or real estate, individuals have the potential to earn higher returns compared to traditional savings accounts. Students should learn about investment options, seek professional advice, and invest early to maximize compounding growth.

Example: Let's say a student starts investing $200 monthly in a retirement account at 25. Assuming an average annual return of 7%, by the time they reach 65, they could potentially accumulate over $800,000. This demonstrates the power of long-term, consistent investing.

Understanding money management, saving, and investing is crucial for students' financial well-being. It enables them to build a secure future, achieve financial independence, and have the means to pursue their dreams. Students should be proactive, learn about personal finance, and make informed decisions that align with their financial goals and aspirations.

CHAPTER 2: MESSAGES FOR GROWNUPS

Message #1: Don't be Quick to Ask, What do You Want to be When You Grow up?

Hey there, grown-ups! We must ease up on bombarding high school students with questions about their future careers. It seems harmless, but trust me, it's time to adopt a more supportive and lighthearted approach. As high school students navigate their educational journey, they often face a barrage of questions from well-meaning adults about their future career plans. While it may seem harmless, constantly asking students what they want to be when they grow up can have unintended negative consequences.

Unrealistic Expectations and the Inferiority Complex: Imagine assuming every student will pursue a four-year degree and conquer the world. It sounds like a fairytale, right? Well, it's time to ditch those unrealistic expectations. By assuming a one-size-fits-all approach, we unintentionally make students feel inadequate or inferior if their dreams don't align with our societal norms. Let's celebrate diversity and acknowledge that there are countless paths to success. When adults assume that all students will attend college and pursue specific career paths, they inadvertently create unrealistic expectations. **Some students may not have the aptitude or desire to pursue a four-year degree, and when adults make assumptions, it can make them feel inadequate or inferior.** It's important to acknowledge that there are diverse paths to success and avoid projecting societal norms onto students with different aspirations.

Decision-Making with a Side of Panic: Ah, high school—the land of self-discovery and exploration. Students are still figuring out their likes, dislikes, passions, and pet peeves. Bombarding them with future-focused questions only adds fuel to the anxiety fire. They're not fortune-tellers! Let's give them the time and space to make informed decisions without pushing them into hasty choices or making up answers to please us. Trust me, nobody wants a world full of reluctant astrophysicists. Many high school students are still in the process of discovering their interests and passions. They may not know what they want to do after graduation, which is normal. **Bombarding them with questions about their future only adds to their anxiety and may push them into making hasty decisions or providing false answers to please others.** It is crucial to give students the time and space to explore their options and make informed decisions based on their interests and abilities.

Authenticity over Approval: Picture this: We ask a student about their plans, and they scramble to give a response that sounds impressive or socially acceptable. It's like watching a poorly scripted movie. We're **promoting conformity over authenticity!** Instead, let's encourage genuine self-discovery and growth. It's time to ditch the pressure to please others and foster an environment that celebrates each student's journey.

The Emotional Rollercoaster: High school is already a rollercoaster ride of emotions. Adding pressure about future careers can turn it into a wild, nausea-inducing loop-de-loop. Students feel embarrassed, anxious, and inadequate if they haven't figured it out yet. Let's be the support system they need, creating an environment that nurtures their self-esteem, mental well-being, and academic performance. Laughter and acceptance go a long way! High school can be a time of intense pressure and stress for students. Students may experience embarrassment, inadequacy, or anxiety if they haven't figured out their career path **when asked about their plans in front of friends and family.** This unnecessary pressure can harm their self-esteem, mental well-being, and academic performance. Adults must create a supportive, non-judgmental environment that encourages open discussions without imposing expectations.

Empowering Conversations: Now, for the fun part! Instead of cornering students with career questions, let's adopt an empowering and supportive stance. Embrace the art of open-ended questions like, "What interests have you been exploring?" or **"How can I assist you in planning your post-high school adventure?"** It's all about giving them space to express themselves without feeling the world's weight on their shoulders. Let's celebrate their unique accomplishments and challenges. This allows students to engage in meaningful conversations about their aspirations without feeling pressured to have all the answers. Adults can acknowledge students' achievements and challenges during their high school journey, showing appreciation for them.

We create an environment that fosters authenticity, personal growth, and laughter by easing up on the career interrogation. High school is a transformative time; we guide, empower, and appreciate each student's path. Let's focus on empowering students, providing guidance when needed, and nurturing an environment where they feel comfortable exploring their interests and making informed decisions about their futures. So, let's ditch the pressure and embrace the joy of nurturing their dreams and aspirations.

Message #2: "Because I Said So" is not Always the Best Answer

Because I said so is indeed the best answer for toddlers, adolescents, and even high school seniors, especially in times of extreme danger. However, if we aim to teach our offspring, we can never ignore their "why" questions. With all they view on television, society, and even our double standards, they have the right to receive an explanation. Furthermore, parents should feel honored if our high school students take the time to ask us why a particular rule was made. It is an opportunity to help them mature, and it can increase your relationship with them. Sometimes, parents have difficulties in maintaining good relationships with their teenage children. This can happen when parents yell or punish to get their point across. However, it is essential to remember that it is not about who is right or wrong. Even if your teenager is wrong, listening to them and acknowledging their feelings is crucial. If you don't, they may feel like their opinions are not valued and will cling to their own beliefs without considering others'. It is essential to have open and honest conversations with your teenager to avoid misunderstandings and maintain a healthy relationship. It is also possible that the teenager is right.

Teenagers will resent you if they cannot express their feelings. Even worse, they will feel stifled and may seek alternate allies to share their feelings with. So, as correct as you were as a parent, you will lose their respect. Think about this: How would you like to talk with your supervisor at work and find that they will not listen to your side? Instead, they tell you everything wrong about what you did; they take your car, cell phone, and all privileges and lock you in the office or the cafeteria.

That doesn't work. And by the way, many students have burner phones.

As a high school counselor working closely with teenagers and their families, I have witnessed the transformative impact of active listening on parent-teen relationships. I've had my fair share of conversations with students who claim their parents don't listen to them. Adolescence is a time of immense growth, self-discovery, and emotional turbulence. During this crucial period, parents play a vital role in creating a supportive environment by actively listening to their teenagers.

Begin with the end in mind. What do you want? Their "crime" is somewhat irrelevant. I know, I know: They were smoking weed, they had sex, they got into a fight, they took on a boyfriend you disapprove of, they failed a test, or some other hideous unforgivable act. It is your job to find out why they (think they) like "that boy" so much, not lock them in a cellar to keep them from the boy. Ultimately, they will break free and possibly make even more wrong choices. It is more important to teach them self-respect than to punish them. If they are repeat offenders who constantly break your rules, that is another story for another book. Teens can be very skillful and manipulative when getting what they want, even if it is bad for them. So, it would be best to have them trust and respect you, not resent you. If they trust and admire you, their chances of listening to and taking your advice will increase. If you don't listen to them, they will not "hear" you.

Message #3: Learn Communicating with Teenagers 101

The Vanishing Chatterbox: Remember when your little one couldn't stop talking? They babbled non-stop about anything and everything. Fast forward to the teenage years, and suddenly, it's like they've taken a vow of silence. Now, I know what you're thinking. Is it just a natural part of growing up? Well, not entirely. It's more about how we, as parents, adapt our communication style over the years.

The Curious Case of Parental Interest: Picture this: You're at the dinner table, and your teenager starts talking about their day at school. But instead of engaging in conversation, you find yourself scrolling through your phone or mentally planning your next grocery trip. Sound familiar? Here's a revelation: Parents, we need to show interest and engage with our children from an early age. It's like keeping the inquisitive flame alive, making them comfortable sharing their thoughts. Adolescents often struggle with feelings of being misunderstood or unheard, leading to strained relationships. By actively listening, you bridge the gap between generations and create an atmosphere of mutual respect. This strengthens the parent-teen connection, fostering open and honest communication, which is crucial for navigating the challenges of adolescence.

Shame, Secrets, and Missed Conversations: Ever wonder why your teenager keeps secrets or acts all mysterious? It's not because they've discovered some ancient teenage code of silence. Nope. It's because we, as parents, stop asking about their lives. When we fail to have those meaningful conversations, they miss out on the chance to talk about things that matter. They start feeling a little shameful about keeping their experiences to themselves, and that's when the real fun begins.

Time to Press the Reset Button: Don't worry, folks. It's not too late to turn things around. Suppose you're thinking, "Where did all those years go without talking to my child?" fear not. We've got solutions! Let's start by meeting them where they are now, in the present. Ask about their day, listen attentively, and resist the urge to butt in with your own stories. Remember, they're testing your interest, so show them you genuinely care.

Games, Laughter, and Connection: Who said parenting couldn't be fun? Playing games like Scrabble or going on long drives can work wonders. Turn off the music and engage in activities that require laughter and collaboration. Trust me, you'll soon see the tension dissipate, and your teenager will feel more comfortable opening up. And don't forget to share your stories and experiences too. It's all about creating a level playing field.

The Art of Non-Judgment: I know it's hard, but resist the urge to judge. Accept your child for who they are, quirks and all. You don't have to be their best friend, but being open-minded and non-judgmental goes a long way. If they feel you trust them and won't jump to conclusions, they'll be more inclined to share their thoughts, fears, and dreams with you.

Empowering Your Teenager's Voice: Teenagers yearn for autonomy and independence as they explore their identities and values. By listening to your teenager, you empower them to voice their opinions, desires, and aspirations. Acknowledging their autonomy helps develop their decision-making skills and fosters a sense of agency. When parents actively listen, they provide a platform for their teenagers to build self-confidence and critical thinking, enabling them to make informed choices.

Enhancing Problem-Solving Skills: Listening attentively to your teenager allows them to express their concerns and challenges. By doing so, parents gain valuable insights into their teenager's world, enabling them to offer guidance and support effectively. Active listening also encourages teenagers to reflect on their own experiences and find solutions to their problems. This empowers them to develop essential problem-solving skills and resilience, fostering independence and self-reliance.

Creating a Supportive Environment for Mental Health: Adolescence is when mental health issues can arise or become more pronounced. By listening to your teenager without judgment, you create a supportive environment for them to discuss their emotional well-being. This helps identify signs of distress or mental health challenges early on, ensuring timely intervention and support. Actively listening to your teenager's concerns can promote emotional well-being, reduce stigma around mental health, and encourage them to seek help when needed.

Practical Strategies for Effective Parental Listening

Practice active listening: Give your teenager your undivided attention, maintain eye contact, and provide verbal and non-verbal cues to show that you are engaged and attentive.

Be non-judgmental: Create a safe space for your teenager to express themselves without fear of criticism or ridicule.

Avoid interrupting or offering immediate solutions: Allow your teenager to fully articulate their thoughts and feelings before providing guidance or advice.

Reflect and paraphrase: Summarize and rephrase what your teenager has shared to ensure you understand their perspective accurately.

Validate their emotions: Show empathy and understanding by acknowledging and validating your teenager's feelings, even if you disagree with their viewpoint.

Conclusion: Listening to your teenager is a powerful way to foster a deep and meaningful connection. By actively listening, parents validate their teenager's experiences, strengthen the parent-teen bond, and empower teens to use their voices. It is not about who is right or wrong. Your teenager might be wrong about an issue, but your failure to listen to their side could decide whether they will ever receive what you have to say or your position. They will feel "unheard." As such, if they have faulty beliefs, they will hold on to them in their heads because they never got the opportunity to have a real conversation about the issue.

Message #4: Use Reading as a Tool

First, I want to highlight how parents can use reading as a "punishment." Now, we know reading is not a punishment -and the time will come when the child thinks he has tricked you because they begin to enjoy reading. For students who already love to read, you can still assign reading what you want them to read. If they break a rule, give them a reading assignment. Watch them attempt to read beyond the time of the "punishment" because they are so engrossed!

This next idea might sound ridiculous, but trust me, it will be worth it. Suppose you have a child in high school, and you either never or no longer read to them. You know, those bedtime stories where you had time together? You would be the last person your child would see at night, and you would strengthen your relationship by reading something peaceful or enjoyable. Or, suppose you have never experienced that. Then do it now. I am being so serious. Grab a book, and schedule a time to read to them in their room before they go to sleep. You may even get more out of it now than when your child was a toddler. And guess what? You don't even have to read all the time. Just tell stories or family jewels. Those might even turn into conversations. Do this before your child leaves home. Or do it when they come for visits. Think of everything you want to tell your child that you still haven't taught them.

Rediscovering the Joy of Reading: Those who claim they don't like reading might just be missing out on the suitable material that sets their souls on fire. Growing up, maybe you didn't have many books or got caught up in the electronic whirlwind. But guess what? Reading is a whole universe, bursting with gripping novels, mind-expanding non-fiction, and everything in between. By exploring different genres and subjects, you might stumble upon a book that grabs hold of your imagination and ignites a lifelong love for reading. Not only is it joyful, but reading is also a necessity.

The Power of Storytelling: Stories have this magical power to transport us to different times, places, and even the minds of others. When we immerse ourselves in narratives, we develop empathy and understand the joys and struggles of human experience. My friends, we all have stories to tell, and reading unlocks our untapped potential as storytellers. By reading and sharing our own stories, we weave together the fabric of our communities, build bridges, and inspire others to embrace the power of reading.

Modeling Reading for the Next Generation: Now, listen up, parents and role models! You all have the superpower to shape the reading habits of our young ones. When we prioritize reading and show our love for it, we set an example that inspires the next generation. It's like dropping a pebble in a pond —the ripples of positive change spread far and wide. So snap a pic of yourself lost in a book or share your latest literary adventures with others. You catalyze awesomeness within your community, inspiring others to join the reading revolution.

So, my dear friends, here's the truth: when you say you don't like reading, chances are you haven't found suitable material or fully realized the incredible benefits of embracing the habit of reading.

.

CHAPTER 3: EMERGENCY TIMELINES AND MORE

Introduction

Most of us do not live in an ideal world where we have things perfectly planned. The good news is that even last-minute planning can have happy endings. Just make up your mind that you are ready to start, and from that point, the postsecondary planning continues. It continues because you have endured being shaped and developed characteristics that will influence your path. This chapter contains multiple variations of timelines. Who are you, and where are you in the planning stages of your future?

If you want to explore interests and get a head start, it is always time (3rd grade, middle school, your junior year...six months old) to explore career paths and examine the best way to get there. But, even if you are a senior who has not made any plans or does not have money for college, it is never too late to start! Just think: Some people make whole career changes in their fifties. Students can always change their minds after setting post-high school plans. Now, ideally, these discussions should start at least by middle school. Gather around the family table or the superhero headquarters and discuss the future and those financial considerations. Let's talk about the cost of college, saving plans, and those magical military benefits. Knowledge is power, my friends, and staying informed and excited about the various routes to finance your future is critical.

No Time for Bickering with Parental/Guardian Stakeholders

Students and parents, let's address the elephant in the room: family dynamics. We know that divorce and other challenging situations can complicate things, but here's the deal—this is not the time for bickering or letting egos take center stage. Nope, not cool. We're all about bringing everyone together, regardless of history. So, if your dad has been missing in action (MIA) or your mom is unbearable-in your opinion, let's put those differences aside and focus on what's best for you.

Remember, postsecondary planning is a team effort. So, put aside the disagreements, bring out your sense of humor, and unite as a united front. Together, navigate the high school journey, make intelligent decisions, and set you up for a bright and prosperous future. Cheers to putting the "fun" in dysfunctional family dynamics!

Whether you have a parent in isolation or going through a divorce, let's put our differences aside and focus on the real hero of this story: the student! If one parent has been absent, no worries! We're assembling a team of mentors, professionals, and role models to help guide our scholars. Doctor uncles, prosperous business people, or even the friendly neighborhood Spiderman – everyone can lend a hand!

Remember, it takes a village to raise a scholar, like a whole Avengers team, to defeat a supervillain.

Let's set aside personal feelings and work together for the greater good. We're talking about conversations, job shadowing opportunities, and ensuring our students benefit from all the nearby resources. And custodial parents, please resist the urge to block growth because of personal feelings. We're all in this together!

So, students and parents, assemble your forces, put aside your differences, and let's embark on this postsecondary planning adventure united! Collaboration is key! Encourage open conversations and job-shadowing opportunities with family members, friends, or professionals who can offer valuable insights. Don't try to be a one-person show! We understand it might be tricky, but let's ensure you benefit from all the nearby resources. Custodial parents, please resist the urge to block growth due to personal feelings. Let's prioritize the scholar's future and open those support channels.

Together, we can conquer any challenge that comes our way, make informed decisions, and pave the path to a bright and prosperous future. Get ready to save the day, one postsecondary plan at a time!

12-month Emergency Timeline for College-Bound High School Seniors

Here's a 12-month emergency timeline for high school seniors who may have procrastinated on preparing for their postsecondary goals:

August-September: The "Panic Mode" Phase. Realize that time is of the essence, and panic sets in. Embrace the chaos with a dramatic sigh and vow to get your act together. Start by listing everything you need to do to avoid a complete meltdown. Consistently check your school email for college and career information and announcements. Know what is going on!

September-October: The "Speed Dating" Phase. Attend college fairs and open houses with the enthusiasm of a speed dater. Collect pamphlets, chat with admissions officers, and devour free snacks. Take notes, but don't forget to impress them with your witty banter. Who knows? You might find "the one."

October: The "Research Frenzy" Phase. Embark on a wild research adventure. Dive deep into the internet rabbit hole and explore potential career paths, colleges, and scholarships. Collect information like a hoarder on a mission, but take breaks to prevent information overload-induced migraines.

The "Application Frenzy" Phase. Channel your inner superhero and conquer those college applications like a pro. Write killer personal statements, showcase your unique qualities, and don't forget to proofread. Attend College Applications Week programs at your school if it is offered. Embrace the art of multitasking by simultaneously stuffing envelopes while binge-watching your favorite TV show.

November: The "Reality Check" Phase. Confront the cold, hard truth that deadlines are looming. Prioritize your choices based on feasibility, interests, and the strength of your procrastination skills. Seek guidance from friends, family, or a wise old owl if you're lucky enough to find one.

November-December: The "Scholarship Hunt" Phase. Embark on a treasure hunt for scholarships. Unleash your inner Sherlock Holmes and scour the internet, community boards, and secret society gatherings for hidden funding opportunities. Remember, even the weirdest scholarships can fund your dreams. Apply for scholarships over the Winter Break.

December: The "Nagging Reminder" Phase. Receive gentle reminders from well-meaning friends, parents, and pets about deadlines. Embrace their relentless nudges and acknowledge their desire to see you succeed. Thank them by showering them with occasional moments of sanity and gratitude.

December-January: The "Waiting Game" Phase. Gracefully enter the world of anticipation to learn whether or not you get accepted and that your multiple scholarship applications render at least one win. Embrace the suspense by learning to juggle, tightrope walk, or speak fluent dolphin. Whatever keeps you distracted and entertained while you await those acceptance letters.

January-February: The "Decision Dilemma" Phase. Celebrate acceptance and dive headfirst into the world of decision-making. Weigh the pros and cons like a master debater, consult your Magic 8-Ball, and seek advice from trusted mentors. Remember, a coin flip is a valid decision-making strategy in times of extreme uncertainty.

March: The "Preparation Panic" Phase. Realize that college is just around the corner, and panic sets in once again. Channel your inner superhero, make to-do lists, and tackle those last-minute preparations. Buy dorm essentials, practice doing laundry, and stock up on enough ramen to feed a small army.

April: The "Senioritis Overload" Phase. Senioritis may kick in, but resist its seductive call. Finish strong academically, attend graduation rehearsals without tripping, and savor the bittersweet moments with friends. It's not over until you've gracefully walked across that stage.

May: The "New Beginnings" Phase. Congratulations, you've survived the chaos! Embrace the excitement of new beginnings, college adventures, and the thrill of stepping into the unknown. Embrace

Now, let's slow it down a bit:

Birth to 8th Grade

Indeed, by middle school, students should be having discussions with parents, guardians, family members--or anyone else who may be assisting with planning for the future and financial considerations. Students should be made aware of the cost of college and saving plans the family might have; students should understand how military benefits work and remain knowledgeable and excited about the various routes available to finance their future. Students and families should save money, explore interests, and explore career options because both items can start before preschool. High school students and parents can begin saving accounts like 529 plans or an Educational Savings Account (ESA) if they did not create a savings plan in the past.

I am underscoring the importance of summer engagements. Don't let a summer pass by without engaging in some uplifting activity, whether spiritual, physical, academic, cerebral, or a personal hiatus where students spend time trying to establish inner peace, as that is indeed a journey. There will be plenty of time left over in the summer to work at a paying job, hang out with friends, and even get into trouble if there is too much idle time. The goal is to use the summers to propel students forward, not backward, or stagnant.

This time is permeated by discussions about postsecondary planning with all family stakeholders involved. Set a Four-Year Plan and academic timeline filled with courses for all four high school years that will help explore the stated career. Explore classes and programs with the opportunity to earn industry credentials, college credit, or internships. The primary career goal path is identified (i.e., trade school, four-year college, straight into the workforce, etc.) The necessity here is that the student is involved in the planning stages.

Timelines for Grades 8-11

6-8th Grade:

- Participate in Community Activities and Volunteerism.
- Explore Academic Camps and Summer Programs.
- Join clubs and organizations on campus that interest you.
- Begin researching careers and colleges online.
- Establish good study habits and academic routines.

8th Grade & 9th Grade:

- Build Strong Relationships: Connect with your teachers, counselors, and mentors. Actively participate in class, ask questions, and seek guidance when needed. Building positive relationships with educators can provide valuable support and recommendation letters in the future.
- Develop Time Management Skills: Use your first year to establish effective time management strategies. Learn how to balance academics, extracurricular activities, and personal commitments. Prioritize tasks, set goals, and create a study schedule to stay organized and productive.
- Explore Interests and Passions: Use your free time to explore different hobbies, activities, and subjects. Attend workshops, seminars, or online courses related to your interests. This helps you gain exposure to various disciplines and discover potential career paths.
- Take practice tests for the PSAT, ACT, and SAT.
- Develop a Four Year Plan.
- Improve Communication and Writing Skills: Use opportunities to enhance your communication and writing abilities. Engage in public speaking activities, join a debate club, or participate in writing contests. These skills are valuable in college applications, essays, and future professional endeavors.

Remember, ninth grade is just the beginning of your journey. Take this time to explore, learn, and lay the foundation for future success. Stay curious, open-minded, and proactive in pursuing your interests and goals.

10th Grade:

- Document Your Service and Experience History: Start an electronic portfolio to track your accomplishments, including volunteer hours, certifications, commendation letters, and other items.
- Deepen involvement in Community Activities and Volunteerism.
- Explore Academic Camps and Summer Programs that align with your interests.
- Step out of your comfort zone and join clubs and organizations to broaden your horizons.
- Take the PSAT standardized test to practice and assess your readiness for the SAT.
- Seek mentorship or guidance from teachers, counselors, or professionals in fields of interest.

- Explore Career Shadowing or Internship Opportunities: Reach out to professionals in fields of interest and inquire about shadowing or internship opportunities. Spending time in a professional setting allows you to gain firsthand experience, observe daily tasks, and make connections in the industry.
- Start Building a Professional Network: Attend career fairs, networking events, or workshops relevant to your areas of interest. Engage in conversations, ask questions, and exchange contact information with professionals you meet. Cultivating a network early on can provide valuable insights, mentorship, and future job prospects.
- Begin Researching Scholarships and Financial Aid: Explore scholarship opportunities and understand the financial aid process. Research local and national scholarships, noting their eligibility criteria and application deadlines. Familiarize yourself with financial aid resources, such as the FAFSA (Free Application for Federal Student Aid), and gather necessary documents for future applications.
- Strengthen Your Academic Profile: Continue to challenge yourself academically by enrolling in advanced or honors courses that align with your interests. Seek opportunities to engage in independent research projects or participate in academic competitions. Consider pursuing extracurricular activities or tasks that demonstrate your passion and commitment in a specific area.

Remember, these actions guide your journey, but balancing preparation and enjoying your high school experience is essential. Be proactive, seek guidance from mentors and counselors, and continue exploring your interests and passions.

11th Grade:

- Continue documenting your accolades and experiences.
- Take on leadership roles in community activities and volunteerism.
- Continue participating in academic camps and summer programs.
- Consider starting an organization on your campus to showcase leadership skills.
- Take the ACT and SAT standardized tests.
- Research and visit colleges, attend college fairs, and schedule campus tours.
- Narrow down your college and career interests.
- Continue exploring scholarship opportunities.
- Seek letters of recommendation from teachers or mentors.
- Pursue advanced courses or Dual Enrollment: Consider enrolling in Advanced Placement (AP) or International Baccalaureate (IB) courses or explore dual enrollment options to earn college credits while in high school. Taking on more rigorous coursework demonstrates your academic capabilities and preparedness for college-level academics.
- Develop Professional Skills: Take the initiative to develop essential professional skills, such as effective communication, problem-solving, and leadership. Engage in activities or workshops focusing on these skills and seek opportunities to apply them in real-world scenarios.
- Engage in Research or Internship Experiences: Look for research programs or internships in fields of interest. Engaging in hands-on research or internships allows you to delve deeper into a specific area, gain practical experience, and strengthen your

college applications or resumes.

- Prepare for College Entrance Exams: Dedicate time to preparing for the ACT or SAT exams. Take practice tests, utilize study resources, or consider joining a test prep program to improve your scores. Additionally, explore any subject-specific tests or exams required for your intended college major or program.
- Explore Career-Specific Opportunities: Delve deeper into your career interests by seeking opportunities that align with your desired field. This could include attending career-specific workshops, participating in relevant competitions, or connecting with professionals through informational interviews or job shadowing experiences.
- Attend College Application Workshops or Seminars: Seek out workshops or seminars offered by your school or local organizations that guide the college application process. Gain insights on crafting solid personal statements, filling out applications, and navigating the admissions process effectively.
- Expand Your Network: Continue to build connections with professionals in your field of interest. Reach out for informational interviews, job shadowing, or mentorship opportunities. Networking can provide valuable insights, advice, and potential career pathways.
- Take on Leadership Roles in School Clubs or Organizations: Aim to secure leadership positions in clubs or organizations you're involved in. These roles showcase your ability to take initiative, collaborate with others, and positively impact your school community.

While it's essential to focus on college and career preparation, it's equally important to maintain a healthy balance with your overall high school experience. Enjoy extracurricular activities, nurture friendships, and take time for self-care. Embrace growth opportunities, explore your interests, and continue developing the skills and knowledge to support your future endeavors.

Summer Before Senior Year

1. Participate in academic or industry camps and summer programs to enhance your skills.
2. Visit the colleges of your choice and narrow down your decision.
3. Attend college and career fairs.
4. Go on tours to visit the industries you want to pursue.
5. Plan and list teachers to ask to write letters of recommendation for you. Equip them with your unofficial transcript and your resume. Two weeks' advance notice is sufficient when requesting a letter, but three weeks is better.

12th Grade Timeline

August-September:

- Visit college and industry reps who come to your high school to learn from them, even if you don't plan on pursuing that route.
- Continue documenting your accolades and experiences.
- Create or update your essay templates for scholarships and cover letters.
- Ask teachers, counselors, club sponsors, community members, etc., for LORs.

- Take on prominent leadership roles in community activities and volunteerism.
- Finalize your college-industry list and submit applications by their respective deadlines.
- Students entering the workforce should pay attention to certifications and exam dates.
- Apply for external scholarships.
- College-bound student-athletes should register with the NCAA/NAIA Clearinghouse. Visit this website: www.eligibilitycenter.org
- Read the Early Action, Early Decision, and regular decision guidelines for the colleges of your choice. Keep this information in mind while applying.
- Take a look at the schools associated with the **Common Application, the Coalition Application, The Black College Application**, and maybe others to determine whether or not you want to apply to multiple schools at a time or apply to the traditional one school at a time manner.
- Apply to either college or your trade program; sign career contracts; otherwise, cement your plans if you are committed to doing so. If you are not ready to commit, begin or restart the **incredible journey of exploration**!

October

- Take any remaining standardized tests required for college admission. Many students take the ACT a final time in October.
- Complete the FAFSA.
- November 1 is a significant college application deadline for some colleges and universities. Plan and make sure you are aware of your school's deadlines.
- Attend college and career fairs, interviews, and campus visits as needed.
- Prepare and submit necessary documents for college enrollment, such as housing applications and health forms.

November

- Estimate your federal financial aid eligibility with the FAFSA4caster.
- November 1 is a significant college application deadline for some colleges and universities. Plan and make sure you are aware of your school's deadlines.
- Early Action or Early Decision: If you are considering any of these, you must usually apply in November, November 1st, or November 15th. This means you will also have to take the ACT or SAT sooner.

December

- Gather Your Acceptance Letters and Compare Financial Aid Packages–
- Submit 30-50 more scholarship applications. You can do this if you are organized and use a spreadsheet. Request to take my scholarship class if you need help.

Early Decision – December

If you applied for Early Decision, it means you have committed to attending the school if your application is accepted. You must submit a deposit soon after receiving your acceptance letter, usually in mid-December. However, if you cannot attend for a valid reason, you may be able to withdraw without any adverse effects. It is essential to have a compelling reason for your withdrawal.

If you are applying for Early Decision II, the deadline is usually January 1st. Not all schools offer this application option, however.

January

- Can you increase your ACT score enough to qualify for a scholarship? Can you meet the deadline for said opportunity if you test in the Spring? If so, consider taking either the ACT or the SAT.
- Review your FAFSA report to see what loans or grants you might qualify for. Go to www.fafsa.ed.gov or call FAFSA at 1-800-433-3243 for more information.
- Examine your recalculated GPA. If it has increased, submit a midyear report to your colleges.

February

Compare the cost of your first college choice with your other options and see if you can come up with a final postsecondary destination decision.

March-April

- Make your final college decision and send in your deposit by the deadline (if required).
- You may be able to apply for your dorm if applicable.
- Obtain a "Dorm Essentials" list and collect the needed items.
- Prepare for graduation and enjoy the rest of your senior year!

May

- National College Decision Day is May 1st.
- Early Action applications are not binding, and students usually have until May 1st to notify the college of their intention to attend. A deposit is also needed by this date.
- Sign up for orientation.
- Check with your collegiate institution's deadlines and complete all admission tasks.
- Submit additional financial aid information directly to the registrar's office at your college (extenuating financial circumstances, etc.)
- Make your final college decision and notify the schools you will not attend.

May-June

- Celebrate your accomplishments and enjoy your last summer of high school!
- Pack and prepare: Make a checklist of essential items to pack for college. Coordinate logistics for moving, transportation, and any other preparations necessary for your smooth transition to college life.
- Stay focused on academics and maintain a strong finish in high school.

Remember, these timelines are flexible, and it's essential to adjust them based on your circumstances and goals. Seek guidance from teachers, counselors, and mentors throughout the process. Embrace the journey, remain proactive, and stay open to new opportunities that may arise. Good luck!

High School to Career Timeline for Seniors

Planning for a career right after high school can be a rewarding choice, and there are several steps 12th-grade senior students can take to prepare for a good-paying job or a career in the workforce. Here's a timeline and some guidance:

12th Grade - Fall Semester:

- Self-assessment: Reflect on your interests, skills, and passions. Consider what careers align with your strengths and what you enjoy doing.
- Research careers: Explore various careers that do not require a college degree. Look into job market trends, salary potential, and growth opportunities.
- Networking: Start networking with family, friends, and acquaintances to learn about potential job openings or internships. Attend local job fairs and career expos.
- Resume development: Create a resume highlighting your skills, experiences, and achievements. Tailor it for the specific jobs or industries you're interested in.

12th Grade - Spring Semester:

- Job search: Begin actively searching for entry-level job openings in your chosen field. Use job search websites, company websites, and local job boards.
- Internships and part-time jobs: If possible, secure internships or part-time jobs related to your career interests. These can provide valuable experience and contacts.
- Skills development: Consider enrolling in vocational or technical courses that enhance your skills and qualifications for your chosen career path.
- Certifications: Research any certificates or licenses required for your desired job and start the process if necessary.

12th Grade - Summer:

Prepare for interviews: Practice your interview skills by answering common questions. Dress professionally and gather references.

After High School Graduation:

Job applications: Continue applying for jobs and attending interviews. Be open to entry-level positions that provide growth opportunities.

Networking: Attend local industry events and join professional organizations related to your field. Networking can lead to job opportunities and career advice.

Financial planning: Create a budget and financial plan to manage your income effectively. Consider saving for further education or training if you decide to advance your career.

Continuous learning: Even if you're not pursuing a traditional college degree, seek ongoing learning and skill development opportunities. Attend workshops, online courses, or community college classes if necessary.

Long-term career goals: As you gain experience in your chosen field, start thinking about your long-term career goals. Consider if additional education or certifications will be beneficial for career advancement.

Remember that each person's career path is unique, and there's no one-size-fits-all approach. Staying adaptable and open to new opportunities as you work toward your career goals is essential. Building a solid work ethic, being professional, and continuously improving your skills will contribute to your success in the workforce.

CHAPTER 4: THE BASIC NECESSITIES

This chapter is significant, scholars. Whenever I thought of authoring this book, the information in this chapter is what I originally wanted to share. Some items here seem...basic (lol), but mastering and understanding their importance can make or break students.

Detecting Senioritis

Ah, Senioritis! That wacky phenomenon that turns even the most diligent students into masters of procrastination and champions of "I'll do it tomorrow." It's like a comedy sketch, with textbooks gathering dust, assignments piling up, and the looming threat of impending deadlines.

Definition of Senioritis: Senioritis is a highly contagious condition that affects students of all ages and academic backgrounds as they approach the end of the school year. It's characterized by an extreme lack of motivation, a sudden fascination with Netflix binges, and a chronic case of "just one more episode" syndrome. Symptoms include a strong desire for freedom, a tendency to daydream about summer vacation, and an uncanny ability to find every excuse to avoid studying or completing assignments.

Solutions for Senioritis

Embrace Your Inner Comedian: Laughter is the best medicine, they say. So why not infuse your study sessions with humor? Create funny mnemonics to remember key concepts, turn notes into silly rhymes, or challenge your friends to a game of academic-themed charades. Finding joy in learning can rekindle your motivation and make studying much more enjoyable.

Break It Down, Comedy Style: Chunking your tasks into bite-sized, laughter-inducing pieces can make them more manageable. Set small goals and reward yourself with funny memes, jokes, or mini-dance parties after completing each. Remember, even the most epic tasks can be conquered with a bit of humor and a lot of silliness.

Form a Senioritis Support Group: You're not alone in this struggle. Gather your fellow senioritis sufferers and form a support group. Share your funniest procrastination stories, exchange tips on combating the lure of laziness, and provide much-needed laughter therapy. Together, you'll find the strength to tackle your tasks while laughing along the way.

Time for a Humorous Study Schedule: Spice up your study routine with comedy. Designate specific time slots for studying, and give each one a funny theme. For example, "The Punniest Hour" could be dedicated to mastering vocabulary, while "Comedy Central Calculus" focuses on solving math problems with a side of laughter. Injecting humor into your schedule can make the process more enjoyable and help you stay focused.

Celebrate Your Achievements: Every completed task is a cause for celebration. Create a humorous reward system for yourself, where each milestone is met with a goofy victory dance, a funny victory speech, or a round of applause from your imaginary audience. By acknowledging your progress and finding joy in your accomplishments, you'll keep the momentum going and overcome Senioritis with a big smile.

Remember, my fellow students, it's essential to find a balance between laughter and responsibility. Stay committed to your goals, harness the power of humor, and tackle your tasks with a lighthearted attitude.

No One Listens to the School Announcements or Reads the Emails

Teachers, keep the students quiet during announcement time! Parents, ask your scholars daily to share what they heard on the school announcements. I've heard why students don't listen to or "Can't hear" the school announcements. Unacceptable, and here is why:

Ignorance Is Not Always Bliss: You might think you're in your little world of TikTok dances and Instagram filters, but guess what? The real world is knocking at your inbox, and it's not taking "I didn't read the email" as an excuse. Those emails hold the secrets to opportunities, deadlines, and important information that can make or break your success. Don't let ignorance be the reason you miss out on life-changing moments.

Baby Boomers Know a Thing or Two: Let's face it, the Baby Boomers have seen some things, and they've got stories to tell. When they send you an email, it's like receiving a message from a wise sage. Sure, their message may not come through to your social media platforms. Baby Boomers might not understand all the latest TikTok trends or Snapchat filters, but they have decades of experience and knowledge to share. So give their emails a chance, and who knows, you might find some pearls of wisdom buried among their paragraphs. It's like getting free life advice, and who can say no to that? Those emails might be from the generation that invented the fax machine, but let's not underestimate their wisdom. They have valuable insights, scholarship details, and advice to shape your future. So put on your "listening ears" (or, in the case of emails, your reading glasses) and give those announcements the attention they deserve. You never know what nuggets of wisdom are waiting to be discovered.

The Mysterious Case of Unopened Emails: Picture this: You're wandering around in a fog of cluelessness, utterly unaware of important events and opportunities passing you by. Meanwhile, your classmates who read their emails are ahead of the game, making informed decisions and getting ahead. It's like being stuck in a parallel universe where missed deadlines and increased stress reign supreme. Don't be the star of this surreal show. Open those emails and join the real world!

The Inbox Treasure Hunt: Think of your email inbox as a hidden treasure chest. Inside those virtual envelopes lie scholarships, internships, and career opportunities waiting to be discovered. It's like a game show where the prize is a brighter future. Each email you open is a step closer to your dreams. So, grab your virtual cape, sharpen your email-reading skills, and let your inbox be the guiding light on your path to greatness.

The $60,000 Email Mishap: Once upon a time, a student had a golden opportunity in their inbox. But alas, they failed to open it, and with a simple click, they lost a $60,000 scholarship. The moral of the story? Don't let a momentary laziness or lack of organization cost you a fortune. Open those emails and follow instructions because you never know what life-changing surprises might await you.

Hush, Hush, It's Announcement Time: Some students complain that their classmates disrupt the classroom during announcements, but that problem needs fixing! Take it up with the school administration and demand some peace. Those daily announcements hold valuable information that can level the playing field. Don't let your classmates have the upper hand just because they're tuned in while you're tuning out. Knowledge is power, my friends!

No Email Escape: Emails have a funny way of finding you, even when you least expect it. Emails represent paper trails.

Remember, school announcements and emails are not just noise and clutter in your life. They are valuable sources of information, opportunities, and connections. By listening attentively and reading those emails, you equip yourself with knowledge, stay on top of important deadlines, and open doors to a world of possibilities. So, be the savvy student who embraces the power of communication because, in the end, it's not just about reading emails—it's about unlocking the key to your success and becoming the hero of your own story.

Email Writing Should be a Part of the Curriculum

Emailing is still a thing despite all the other fancy ways we communicate. It's like the OG method of passing info around! Oh, email, the ancient digital communication art that refuses to die! Despite all the fancy ways we can talk to each other these days, email still reigns supreme as the go-to method for sharing information. But wait, don't hit that "send" button just yet, my dear high schoolers! Crafting an email is no joke. It's like building the foundation for a solid working relationship. And trust me, you don't want to start on the wrong foot and annoy your teachers or future employers with your email antics. So, let's break it down, shall we?

First things first, we've got the "To" section, the "From" section, and oh, that glorious "Subject Line." Think of the subject line as a sneak peek of what's inside the email. Don't try to squeeze your entire message in there, okay? We don't want people squinting at their screens, trying to decode your cryptic subject line. Please give them a hint, not a novel!

Oh, here's a pro tip: The body of your email goes inside the email, not in the subject line! Now, the real action happens in the body of the email. This is where you spill all the juicy information you want to share.

But hold up, buddy, pay attention to your tone! Remember those fancy apps with happy or mean faces? They're not just for fun. They can save your email from becoming a disastrous mess. Take a moment to reassess that email and ensure you're not unintentionally coming across as the next Shakespearean insult master. Seriously, though, the tone of your email is a big deal. No one likes a message that sounds like a robot wrote it. So be polite and friendly, and don't just focus on what you want. It's a conversation, not a demand letter!

Your mom may not appreciate it if you declare her your secretary and give her access to your school accounts. Sorry, students, but it's time to start caring for your business. You're adults now, apparently.

But hey, why does all this email stuff matter? If you try to cram your entire message into the subject line, you'll look like a digital contortionist. Keep it neat, organized, and pleasant to read. And please, don't accidentally insult your recipient. We're aiming for friends, not frenemies!

When you finally hit that "compose" button, don't forget to address the person you're writing to.

Starting an email with "I need you to do this for me" is a no-no. Instead, try something like, "Dear Mr. Green, I hope this email finds you well. So, Mr. Green, my application for the University of Emailification was rejected. Can you be my hero and help me with the appeal process?"

It's OK to send a thank-you email to someone who wrote you a killer recommendation letter. Politeness never goes out of style!

Remember, an email is a legal document, people. Use it responsibly. And don't forget to check your inbox regularly! Your email is like your responsibility, buddy. It keeps you in the loop with what's happening, reduces your stress levels, and makes you feel warm and fuzzy because you're on top of things.

So, my young email aficionados, master the art of email writing and conquer the digital world one witty message at a time. Now, go forth and send those emails like the clever high school scholars you are!

Geesh! Learn how to Write Your Name

Let's discuss the captivating art of adequately signing your name. It truly is a mind-boggling phenomenon that some of you either don't know how to or don't believe it's worth the effort. Allow me to indulge in one of my delightful pet peeves: students who decide to grace forms with their middle name, as if I, your humble counselor, can instantly recall all 600 of you by heart. Oh, and let's not forget those who have a fondness for entering their oh-so-adorable nicknames. It's riveting, isn't it?

But wait, there's more! Witness the marvelous technique of scribbling one's name as if they were auditioning for a modern art masterpiece. Oh, the joy of trying to decipher those barely visible pencil strokes! And let us not overlook the genius minds among us who possess hyphenated last names yet struggle to determine which name should have the grand privilege of going first. Such trivial matters, you say? Ah, but let me regale you with tales of my adventures searching through vast databases, desperately hunting for elusive student identities. All because, you know, it might involve something mildly important like a field trip form or some other mundane document.

My time is precious, dear students, and I must confess it is not delightful or fulfilling to waste it on deciphering your cryptic scribbles. You see, it's a tad frustrating when I cannot approve your participation in an exciting trip simply because I cannot unravel the enigma of your name.

So, my high school compatriots, I beseech you, nay, implore you to embark on a grand expedition of maturity and take responsibility for filling in your information with utmost clarity. Master the art of printing your name, and let your penmanship shine like a beacon of organizational bliss.

Teachers are People, Too

I've got some wisdom to share about the importance of making friends with the "old folks" at school. And "old folks" means the teachers and authority figures in charge right now.

I know you Gen Z students aren't always big fans of rules, and that's understandable. But here's the deal: for now, the Baby Boomers are running the show. And trust me, it would be such a shame if all you brilliant rule-breakers ended up in a sticky situation like prison or missing out on higher education opportunities.

So, here's my advice to you clever students: Take some time to learn and understand the rules quickly. Please try to follow them unless they conflict with your religious beliefs. It might seem like a bit of a drag, but obeying those in authority over you is pretty crucial until you take over the world (sooner than you can imagine!).

Now, here's the thing: Teachers aren't always perfect. Shocking, I know! But if you discover that they may not have all the answers or they make some mistakes, cut them some slack. They're human, too! Try to learn everything you can from them, even if it goes beyond the academic stuff. Never miss out on an opportunity to learn from someone just because you notice a flaw or two in their armor.

Okay, let's talk about being resourceful. Indeed, resourcefulness sometimes requires pushing the boundaries and thinking outside the box. I get it. But in a public high school setting, there's still fear and resistance towards fearless students who don't fit neatly into any box. Some teachers still believe they should always be the ones who know more than their students and keep them in check.

So, here's a question: Who are the people and offices that can help you successfully navigate your high school years? Well, let me tell you. The teachers, counselors, and other school staff are the same "old folks" we discussed earlier. They're there to support you, guide you, and make your journey smoother. Don't hesitate to seek their help and build relationships with them. Trust me, it'll make your high school experience so much better!

Remember, you are the future leaders who will shape the world. But before you take over, it's essential to play by the rules (mostly) and make allies with those who can help you along the way. Keep being awesome, my friends, and embrace the knowledge and guidance available to you. You've got this!

Transcripts

Every year, seniors seek the answer to the question, "How do I get my transcript?" Despite being informed, many struggle to retain this crucial information that affects their education and plans. Students should have a copy of their baseline GPA by tenth grade, as transcripts represent their academic journey and can leave room for assumptions.

This is why essays, letters of recommendation, and resumes are equally important - they offer more insight and can explain any inconsistencies in grades. Even if a student's transcripts reflect perfect grades, recruiters, scholarship committees, and college admissions counselors will look for more than just grades. Therefore, students need to be larger than their transcripts; transcripts with poor grades do not define them entirely.

It is vital to understand each school's procedure for requesting transcripts and order them as soon as possible. Transcripts are so important that schools can hold them hostage if a student has lost a textbook or owes fees, knowing that the need for transcripts will prompt them to respond to financial bills.

Make SURE the College Counselor Knows You

During an event for juniors in the College and Career Center for one week, I met a lively young lady who asked many questions and gave plenty of answers. I had never seen her before -or so I thought. I had passed her probably 3-4 times every school day, but I never *saw* her. With almost two thousand students in the building, I see students in the local markets and do not always recognize them, especially if we have never personally interacted.

So, anyway, I often get opportunities to select a few students for a program. This is not easy. Sometimes, I must run a current roster that matches specific demographics, grade point averages, personalities, and interests. Then, I have to interview my pool to determine the best fit. Other times, I can think of the best-fitted student right off the top of my head. You guessed it: I can do so more readily if I know the student. This young lady made it to my memory bank by interacting with me casually. She would be considered, then.

Students who extend themselves, volunteer their services, or volunteer to answer questions can become more memorable to teachers and counselors in some aspects.

Here's a little secret: It's often the same few students who constantly seek the counselor's time and resources. But guess what? That leaves a lot of students—around 90%—who never bother seeking help. And that can make you feel invisible, especially in larger schools. So, don't be part of that 90%! Step up and make use of the resources available to you.

Now, I know it's easy for us adults to assume that you know everything like the Common App or the Black College App. Or that you're familiar with the characteristics of a liberal arts school. But the truth is, you might not know these things unless you actively seek out information. That's where the College and Career Centers come in.

These centers are treasure troves of resources and opportunities to learn about the postsecondary process. Attending events held in the career center can significantly broaden your perspective. For example, imagine attending a scholarship workshop and discovering that you can apply for scholarships starting as early as sophomore year or hearing a college representative speak for the first time. These experiences can be eye-opening!

Another great benefit is that industry representatives often visit the center, allowing you to learn directly from professionals in different fields. Now, if your school doesn't have a designated center, don't worry. Your senior counselor will likely act in that role and be the liaison between you and your transition from high school.

So, my dear students, don't let yourself fade into the background. Take charge of your future by utilizing the resources available to you. Seek guidance, attend events, and be proactive in college and career exploration. Remember, your high school years are a stepping stone to a fantastic future. You've got this, and your school is here to support you every step of the way!

CHAPTER 5: GOING TO COLLEGE WITH AN IEP OR A 504

Individualized Education Plans (IEPs) and 504 plans are designed to provide support and accommodations to students with disabilities, but they serve slightly different purposes and are governed by other laws. To determine which method is more appropriate for your situation, you should consider your specific needs and consult with the college's disability services office or admissions office.

Here are some critical differences between IEPs and 504 plans:

IEP (Individualized Education Plan):

IEPs are typically developed for students with disabilities in K-12 education settings under the Individuals with Disabilities Education Act (IDEA).

They are more comprehensive and can include specialized instruction, related services, and annual goals.

IEPs are legally binding documents that require schools to provide specific services and accommodations.

IEPs are not typically used in post-secondary education, including colleges and universities, although some colleges may consider them as part of the documentation for accommodations.

504 Plan (Section 504 of the Rehabilitation Act):

504 plans provide accommodations and support to individuals with disabilities in various settings, including colleges and universities.

They are typically less comprehensive than IEPs and focus on equal access to education and services.

Colleges and universities are required to provide reasonable accommodations to students with disabilities under Section 504.

To be eligible for a 504 plan, you must have a qualifying disability that substantially limits one or more major life activities, including learning.

When transitioning from K-12 to college, it's common for students with disabilities to shift from an IEP to a 504 plan or to provide documentation of their disability to request accommodations directly from the college's disability services office. Like those in other states, colleges in Alabama have disability services offices that can help determine the appropriate accommodations based on your needs and documentation.

Here are the steps you can take:

Contact the disability services office at the college(s) you are interested in attending. They can guide their specific procedures and requirements.

Provide documentation of your disability. This may include medical records, evaluations, or documentation of your IEP, if applicable.

Work with the disability services office to discuss your specific needs and develop a plan for accommodations.

Ultimately, the choice between an IEP and a 504 plan may not be applicable at the college level, as colleges typically focus on providing reasonable accommodations to ensure equal access to education for students with disabilities. It's essential to contact the college's disability services office to initiate the process and determine the best course of action for your situation.

CHAPTER 6: STRAIGHT TO THE WORKFORCE FROM HIGH SCHOOL

What it Could Mean in Today's Society

Some high school graduates choose and are sometimes forced to dive into the workforce instead of taking the traditional college route. All races of students who skip training after high school, especially those who fall within lower socioeconomic brackets, may need to brace themselves for waves of limited pay, unequal opportunities, and the occasional shipwreck. You may be aware that the Supreme Court of the United States (SCOTUS) just reached a ruling that has dismantled affirmative action acceptance into colleges and universities. Because of this, it is highly likely that a relationship between that decision and rejected college admission will disparagingly present itself.

Before I list the advantages and disadvantages of high school to the crew, let's keep it 100 and have an honest conversation about this. It should be by design and not by circumstance that one would enter the workforce.

I say to students with no definite plans yet going straight into the workforce, hold on to your life jackets because it's a doggy-dog peddling world out there!

Of course, you can go straight into the workforce right after high school. College is not for everyone; some students need a gap year to work before college. In addition, many jobs would support one's decision to go straight to work. This chapter lists several reasons why it would be practical for some students to head straight into the workforce.

Diversity and Disparities: A Topsy-Turvy World:

In our ideal world, opportunities would rain down on everyone equally, like a shower of gold coins. However, the reality resembles a torrential downpour that conveniently skips over certain groups. African American high school graduates often face the cloudiest skies, with limited access to well-paying jobs and career advancements. It's as if someone handed them an umbrella full of holes. How thoughtful!

Picture this: A student of any ethnicity fresh out of high school, bright-eyed and brimming with ambition and dreams, ventures into the uncharted territory of going straight into the workforce. Others are scared, depressed, or even being asked to leave their homes once they turn 18 or graduate, whichever comes first. They choose or are forced by circumstances to bypass the traditional college route and enter the workforce immediately. Nonetheless, they will conquer the world armed with their diploma or less. They enter the workforce enthusiastically, only to be adrift in a sea of limited pay. The sad truth is that so-called African-American high school graduates often face lower starting salaries than their college-educated counterparts of other races. It's like being handed a paper boat while others are gifted yachts. This is not always due to race alone but rather adverse living situations that disproportionately plague minorities in the United States. Fair winds and following seas, huh?

The Career Ladder

Ah, the career ladder – a rickety construction where hard work and talent should lead to glorious promotions- often seems coated in an invisible layer of grease. Climbing becomes an uphill battle, filled with slippery discrimination, biased hiring practices, and the occasional broken rung. It's almost like trying to ascend Mount Everest with a pair of flippers. Good luck with that!

While it's true that some jobs can support going straight into the workforce, it often becomes a reality for those who find themselves unprepared or trapped in low-paying, dead-end jobs. Sometimes, the allure of fast food employment lures them in, and they unwittingly embark on a spiraling trip toward financial hardship. The McStruggle is real!

Lack of Planning: A Rocky Shoreline:

Aside from the Scotus' decision that could adversely impact collegiate acceptance for minorities, another reason a student may opt for the workforce straight out of high school is a lack of planning. It's as if they suddenly wake up in a romantic movie, complete with a set of children, a newfound love, and a mortgage to pay. But let's face it: not everyone is cut out for college, and some may need a gap year to work and figure things out. However, securing stable employment poses challenges when entering the workforce without particular skills or training beyond high school. It's like searching for a needle in a haystack, blindfolded. I always mention exceptions in this rapidly changing digital and social media world where students can become rock stars overnight if they know how to leverage social media accounts to generate revenue. Regardless of its stability, this area is a new financial opportunity for Gen Z.

The Sinking Ship: Lifetime Earnings Disparities:

These disparities in pay and opportunities can lead to a lifetime of financial struggles for disadvantaged high school graduates. Throughout their careers, the wage gap expands into a vast ocean of lost earnings, making it harder to stay afloat financially. It's like trying to bail water out of a sinking ship with a thimble. Sisyphean, isn't it?

Socioeconomic Background: A Charting Tool:

To truly understand the disparities, we must consider the socioeconomic backgrounds of those entering the workforce. Are they first-generation college students? What is their potential for growth in their chosen field? If we find disparities among socioeconomically disadvantaged individuals or those without a clear plan for upward mobility, Houston, we have a problem.

Ten Potential Advantages of Entering the Workforce Straight Away

Here are ten potential advantages of entering the workforce directly after graduating from high school:

1. **Immediate income:** By entering the workforce, you can earn money immediately and become financially independent. This can be particularly beneficial if you have financial responsibilities or wish to save for future endeavors.
2. **Practical experience:** Work experience provides practical skills and knowledge that can be valuable in the job market. You'll gain hands-on experience and learn how to navigate

real-world work environments.

3. **Early career advancement**: Starting your career early means you have more time to gain experience, build a solid professional network, and potentially advance faster than if you pursued higher education first.

4. **Avoid student debt:** Choosing not to pursue higher education immediately after high school prevents student loans or other financial burdens associated with obtaining a college degree.

5. **Networking opportunities**: Entering the workforce exposes you to a diverse range of professionals who can serve as valuable connections, mentors, or references in the future. Building a solid professional network early on can open doors to new opportunities.

6. **Entrepreneurial opportunities**: You can explore entrepreneurial endeavors or start your own business with more time and freedom. This can provide independence, flexibility, and the chance to pursue your vision.

7. **Immediate contribution:** By joining the workforce, you can directly impact and contribute to the economy, company, or community. This can provide a sense of purpose and fulfillment.

8. **Personal growth:** Work experiences often challenge you to develop crucial skills such as time management, problem-solving, and communication. These skills can contribute to personal development and self-confidence.

9. **Flexibility in career exploration:** Rather than committing to a specific field of study right after high school, entering the workforce allows you to explore different career paths and industries. You can gain insight into your interests and strengths before making long-term commitments.

10. **Potential for advancement without a degree**: Many industries value practical experience and skills over formal education. By starting your career early, you may find opportunities for improvement based on merit and experience rather than relying solely on academic qualifications.

It's important to note that deciding to enter the workforce immediately after high school or pursue higher education should be based on individual circumstances, goals, and aspirations. Both paths have their advantages, and it's crucial to consider your interests, career goals, and long-term plans.

Fifteen Potential Disadvantages For Entering the Workforce Straight Away

Here are 15 potential disadvantages for students who enter the workforce directly after high school without any additional training or certificates:

1. **Limited job opportunities:** Your job options may be limited without specialized training or higher education. Many professions require specific qualifications or certifications beyond a high school diploma.

2. **Lower earning potential:** On average, individuals with a higher level of education tend to earn more over their lifetimes compared to those with only a high school diploma. According to the U.S. Bureau of Labor Statistics, in 2020, the median weekly earnings for someone with a bachelor's degree were $1,305, compared to $746 for someone with only a high school diploma.

3. **Lack of career mobility**: Advancement opportunities may be limited without further

education or training. Higher-level positions often require specialized knowledge or qualifications that a high school diploma may not fulfill.

4. **Higher unemployment rates**: According to the U.S. Bureau of Labor Statistics, as of June 2021, the unemployment rate for individuals with only a high school diploma was 5.8%, compared to 3.1% for those with a bachelor's degree or higher. This indicates that individuals without additional education may face higher unemployment rates.

5. **Limited job security:** Industries and job roles can become obsolete or automated in a rapidly changing job market. Adapting to changing job market demands may be more challenging without further education or training.

6. **Difficulty competing with higher-educated candidates:** When applying for jobs, individuals with higher education or specialized training may have a competitive edge over those with only a high school diploma. This can make it more challenging to secure desirable positions.

7. **Limited access to professional networks:** Higher education often provides opportunities to connect with professionals, professors, and alums who can offer valuable networking connections. Without these networks, finding mentors or job referrals may be more challenging.

8. **Reduced job benefits:** Individuals with only a high school diploma may have limited access to job benefits such as healthcare coverage, retirement plans, or paid leave. Higher education can often lead to better job benefits.

9. **Limited personal growth opportunities:** Higher education offers a broader range of academic and personal growth experiences, such as exposure to different perspectives, critical thinking skills, and unique development opportunities. Without pursuing further education, individuals may miss out on these experiences.

10. **Difficulty changing career paths**: If you enter the workforce without additional training or education, changing career paths later on may be more challenging. Certain industries may require specific qualifications or credentials that you lack.

11. **Impact on future promotions and raises:** Without specialized training or certifications, you may be overlooked for promotions or salary raises compared to colleagues with higher levels of education or additional qualifications.

12. **Increased risk of job dissatisfaction:** Limited job options and the potential for being stuck in low-paying or unsatisfying positions can contribute to job dissatisfaction. This can negatively impact overall well-being and motivation.

13. **Reduced job stability during economic downturns:** During economic recessions or downturns, individuals with higher levels of education tend to experience lower unemployment rates and have a better chance of job security compared to those with only a high school diploma.

14. **Difficulty pursuing certain professions:** Some professions, such as medicine, law, engineering, or teaching, require higher education and specialized training. You may not be eligible for those careers without following these educational pathways.

15. **Missed personal and intellectual development:** Higher education provides opportunities for personal growth, critical thinking, and exposure to various subjects and perspectives. Without further education, you may miss these intellectual and emotional development experiences.

It's important to note that these disadvantages are not absolute, and individual circumstances may vary. Some individuals can find success and fulfillment in their careers without pursuing higher education. However, it's essential to consider the challenges and limitations that may arise from entering the workforce directly after high school without additional training or certifications.

CHAPTER 7: YOUR ESSAY: YOU WERE NOT JUST A BABYSITTER.

Hey there, future scholarship conquerors and college conquerors! So, you're on the journey of snagging scholarships or impressing colleges, right? And guess what? Your regular old report card, test scores, and membership in the "Mathletes Society of the Perpetually Confused" can't truly capture the incredible, unique individual you are. They fall short, like trying to fit into your little cousin's shoes. But fear not! Your trusty sidekick, the essay, is here to save the day!

The Power of the Mighty Essay

Now, let's unravel why your essay is your VIP pass to Scholarville or College Town. Numbers on a transcript or test sheet are like boring, monotone textbooks that put you to sleep faster than a lullaby. Your GPA might be impressive, but it's just a snapshot. Your test scores might be off the charts, but they don't reveal your secret dance moves or your uncanny ability to jump off the roof of a barn and then turn flips. The things that make you who you are must be expressed in your essay.

Enter the essay! It's like your spotlight moment, where you can shine brighter than a supernova. This is where you weave your story, quirks, passions, and dreams into a tapestry of "Oh wow, this person is *incredible*!" Think of your essay as a magic potion that transforms you from a bunch of numbers and achievements into a real, living, breathing legend.

Creativity, Baby!

Now, let's talk about jobs. You know, those things you do to fund your daily doses of caffeine and those rare moments of online shopping therapy? But here's the trick: don't just list your job like a grocery list. "Babysitter" sounds as exciting as plain oatmeal on a rainy day. So, let's give it a makeover, shall we?

Meet "The Toddler Whisperer" – yup, that's you! You *managed the care* of these tiny, adorable dictators who ruled your world with sticky hands and unyielding curiosity. You were the CEO of "Giggles and Crayons Inc.," where you expertly juggled tantrums, crayon catastrophes, and cookie negotiations. You provided a haven for tiny humans while their parents conquered the adult world. Impressive, right?

Choose Words Like a Word Wizard

When crafting your essay, think of yourself as a word wizard, conjuring spells of vivid imagery and intrigue. Instead of "helping out at the local animal shelter," you "dedicated your weekends to the noble mission of cuddling, feeding, and finding forever homes for our four-legged furry friends."

Remember, it's all about showcasing your awesomeness. So, whether you were a "janitorial assistant" or a "mess minimizer," or you "assisted customers" or "crafted unforgettable shopping experiences," sprinkle that fairy dust of creativity all over your experiences.

So, dear future scholarship nabber and college impresser, remember this: your essay is your golden ticket. It's the key to unlocking the door to your dreams and showing the world what an extraordinary human you are. Leave those mundane job titles at the door and embrace your inner word wizard. Let your personality sparkle, your accomplishments shine, and your dreams take center stage. Now go forth, pen in hand, and create an essay masterpiece with scholarships and colleges bowing at your brilliance!

Crafting a Compelling Scholarship Essay:

Introduction

Scholarships offer a golden opportunity for high school students to alleviate the financial burden of higher education. While academic achievement and extracurricular involvement significantly secure scholarships, a well-crafted essay can set you apart from the competition. This section will explore the critical elements of writing an impactful scholarship essay and provide examples of common essay prompts.

Body

**1. ** Understanding the Purpose of the Scholarship Essay

Before delving into the specifics, it's crucial to grasp the purpose of the scholarship essay. Essentially, this essay provides a platform to showcase your unique qualities, experiences, and aspirations that make you an ideal candidate for the scholarship. It's an opportunity to express your story beyond mere grades and achievements.

**2. ** Choosing the Right Topic

Selecting a compelling topic is one of the first steps in crafting a victorious scholarship essay. You may be given a specific prompt or the freedom to choose a topic that aligns with your strengths and experiences. For instance, if the scholarship is focused on community service, you could share a personal anecdote about a meaningful volunteer experience that highlights your dedication and impact.

**3. ** Creating a Strong Introduction

The introduction of your essay is your chance to grab the reader's attention and provide a glimpse of what the essay will cover. A powerful introduction can be achieved through a thought-provoking question, a relevant quote, or a captivating anecdote. For instance, if you are authoring an essay on your career aspirations, you might begin with a quote from a renowned professional.

**4. ** Showcasing Your Achievements and Experiences

The body paragraphs should delve into your achievements, experiences, and qualities that demonstrate why you deserve the scholarship. Utilize concrete examples and vivid descriptions to illustrate your points. If you're discussing your leadership skills, recount a specific instance where you took charge of a project or a team, showcasing your ability to inspire and guide others.

**5. ** Connecting Your Goals to the Scholarship

Another critical aspect is establishing a clear connection between your aspirations and the scholarship you're applying for. If the scholarship is geared toward STEM majors, explain how your passion for science developed and how this scholarship will enable you to further your studies and contribute to the field. Offer specific insights into how the scholarship aligns with your long-term goals.

**6. ** Crafting a Memorable Conclusion

Conclude your essay by summarizing the main points and reiterating your suitability for the scholarship. Leave a lasting impression by reflecting on your journey and expressing gratitude for the opportunity to be considered. You could end with a hopeful statement about the scholarship's impact on your future endeavors.

Common Scholarship Essay Prompts

Personal Statement: Reflect on a personal experience that shaped your character and values, and explain how it has influenced your academic and career goals.

Leadership and Community Involvement: Describe when you demonstrated leadership skills and how you plan to use those skills to impact your community positively.

Overcoming Challenges: Share a significant challenge and detail how you overcame it, emphasizing the lessons learned and your resilience.

Diversity and Inclusion: Discuss the importance of diversity in education and society and share how your unique background fosters inclusivity.

Career Goals: Outline your career aspirations, the steps you've taken to work towards them, and how the scholarship will help you achieve your goals.

Conclusion

Writing a compelling scholarship essay requires careful planning, introspection, and a genuine representation of your unique qualities. By selecting a captivating topic, highlighting your achievements, and effectively connecting your goals to the scholarship's purpose, you can create an essay that leaves a lasting impression on the selection committee. As you embark on this journey, remember that your essay is not just about winning a scholarship but also an opportunity to share your story and inspire others.

CHAPTER 8: THE TRUTH ABOUT LETTERS OF RECOMMENDATION

The ABCs of Asking for a Letter of Recommendation: Avoiding Awkwardness and Achieving Admiration

The thing about letters of recommendation (LOR) is that minors who want to climb ahead need them, so they don't always understand how it works. This is because students often believe that what they need will automatically be provided by adults without any effort or commitment from them. After all, it is not the student's fault that they need these letters! The meaning of letters of recommendation, how to ask, who to ask, and how to prepare to ask is not taught to students. We expect them to know all this, and then stunning letters magically fall out of the sky. Well, there is a science to asking for letters. The first thing is understanding the importance of the letter: A bad LOR can cause a student to miss out on scholarship dollars by the tens of thousands. With that being said, should a student handle asking for a letter in an unprofessional, unappreciative, hasty way? The recommender, the writer, can understand how vital the LOR is to the student based on how the student approaches the request. Thus, the approach can impact the quality of the letter.

A is for Advance Notice: The "Hey, I Need a LOR in Five Days" Epidemic

Ah, yes, the classic student move: waiting until the eleventh hour to ask for a letter of recommendation. Picture this: your professor, bleary-eyed from grading papers, surrounded by a stack of textbooks taller than Mount Everest, and then, out of nowhere, your email appears: "Hey, can you write me a letter of recommendation? Thanks!"

Now, we're all about spontaneity, but if you want your LOR, consider giving your professor a heads-up that doesn't involve a psychic awakening.

B is for Being Specific: The "I Need a LOR, You Know, For Stuff" Syndrome

Dear students, when you request a letter of recommendation, please provide context. Asking for "general" advice doesn't cut it. Imagine a chef preparing your meal based solely on "food" as your order. Be specific about what you're applying for so your letter can be as tailored as a suit.

C is for Not Cute if Your Mom Requests the LOR For You

Picture this: a motherly figure swooping in, clad in superhero attire, demanding, "Write a letter of recommendation for my precious pumpkin, stat!" While we admire a parent's undying love, it's better if you, the student, take the initiative. Professors don't want to be caught in a tug-of-war between parental pride and student ambition.

D is for Documentation: The Case of the Missing Resume

Imagine this scenario: your professor receives an email requesting a letter of recommendation for someone they vaguely remember from a lecture two years ago. The catch? No resume, no supporting documents, just an empty plea.

It's like trying to bake a cake without flour or eggs – sure, you'll get something, but it won't be delicious. Provide your professor with a resume or relevant information so they can craft a recommendation that truly showcases your shining achievements.

E is for Etiquette: The Ghost of "Thank You"

Congratulations, you've secured that coveted letter of recommendation! But hold on – don't pop the celebratory confetti just yet. Sending a heartfelt "thank you" after your professor has gone the extra mile to write that letter is akin to adding the cherry to your academic sundae. You will need him again, and they will remember you didn't show appreciation the first time.

F is for Face-to-Face: The Awkward "Stranger Things" Moment

Picture this: you're asking a professor you've never met for a letter of recommendation. It's like Netflix asking your neighbor's dog to recommend a show. Before you embark on the difficult journey of LOR requests, ensure you've at least shared a nod in the hallway or a knowing glance in the lecture hall. It'll save you from writing, "Dear Stranger, please validate my existence."

In conclusion, dear students, remember that asking for a letter of recommendation isn't just a mere formality. It's a chance for your high school teachers and professors to showcase your brilliance. So, next time you draft that email, channel your inner Shakespeare, be specific, show appreciation, and give your professors enough time to work their magic. Who knows, you might get a recommendation to make your mom proud (and she won't even have to ask for it)!

Recommendation Request Etiquettes

Here's a list of etiquette to follow when asking for a letter of recommendation:

1. Plan Ahead: Give your recommenders plenty of notice, ideally at least 3-4 weeks before the deadline. This allows them enough time to write a thoughtful and well-crafted letter.

2. Choose Wisely: Select recommenders who know you well and can speak to your skills, accomplishments, and character. Quality matters more than quantity.

3. Personal Interaction: Ask in person or via video call whenever possible. If face-to-face isn't possible, send a polite and well-written email.

4. Provide Context: Explain why you're seeking the recommendation and provide details about the position, program, or scholarship you're applying for. This helps your recommender tailor the letter to your specific goals.

5. Share Relevant Information: Supply your recommender with your resume, transcripts, personal statement, or any other relevant materials that can help them write a comprehensive letter.

6. Articulate Your Achievements: Briefly remind your recommender about your achievements and experiences in their class or under their supervision. This will jog their memory and make your request more personalized.

7. Be Respectful of Time: Acknowledge your recommender's busy schedule and ask if they are willing and able to write a strong letter for you. Respect their decision if they decline due to time constraints or lack of familiarity.

8. Follow Guidelines: If the application has specific guidelines for recommendations (format, submission process, etc.), communicate those details to your recommender.

9. Be Courteous and Grateful: Use polite language in your request and express genuine gratitude for their willingness to write the letter on your behalf.

10. Offer an Out: Include a gracious statement that it's okay if they cannot write the recommendation. This shows understanding and eliminates any sense of obligation.

11. Keep It Professional: Even if you have a personal relationship with your recommender, maintain a professional tone in your communication and request.

12. Provide Deadlines: Clearly state the deadline for submitting the recommendation and any necessary details about where and how to present it.

13. Follow Up Politely: If your recommender agrees, send a gentle reminder a week or a few days before the deadline. They may have multiple letters to write and appreciate the prompt reminder.

14. Stay Updated: Inform your recommender if you make any significant updates to your application or receive any offers or invitations related to your application.

15. Send a Thank-You: Once the recommendation is submitted, send a heartfelt thank-you note expressing your appreciation for their support.

Remember, the key is to approach the request with professionalism, courtesy, and gratitude. A well-crafted request and respectful behavior can go a long way in ensuring you receive solid and meaningful letters of recommendation.

CHAPTER 9: BEING RESOURCEFUL IS A GAME CHANGER

Understanding What it Truly Means

Not being resourceful is noticeable and could decide whether you get promoted or offered leadership positions. Experts say that being resourceful may require us to bend some rules. Being resourceful means exploring new areas and pushing boundaries. For students, executive functioning skills are important for managing their daily tasks and self-regulation. But it's also important to teach students the broader concept of resourcefulness by guiding them on how to set goals. This gives them the necessary skills and mindset to handle obstacles, tackle problems, and excel in different aspects of life.

Being resourceful is a vital skill that extends beyond high school and into the real world. It means relying on ourselves, thinking creatively, and finding solutions even in challenging situations.

Real-World Survival: High school is a training ground for life's challenges. It's a microcosm of the real world. Just like being dropped in the middle of a strange city or a foreign country, you may find yourself in unfamiliar situations where you must navigate independently. Being resourceful means assessing the situation, making informed decisions, and taking the necessary steps to adapt and find your way.

Figuring Things Out: Imagine you find yourself in New York City with an appointment to attend that afternoon. Being resourceful means using your problem-solving skills to determine the best way to get there. It might involve using public transportation, finding maps or directions, or asking locals for guidance. The key is to tap into available resources and explore different options to reach your goal.

Embracing New Challenges: Resourcefulness is particularly valuable when faced with new and unfamiliar challenges. Suppose you were suddenly promoted to a job without prior experience; being resourceful means learning, adapting, and seeking the necessary knowledge and skills. You might research, ask for colleague guidance, or use training opportunities to bridge the gap and succeed in your new role.

Understanding Purpose and Requirements: Whether it's in school or the workplace, understanding your purpose and what is expected of you is crucial. Just as students need to know why they are in school and what documents they need to satisfy their involvement, employees must clearly understand their role and the requirements of their jobs. Resourcefulness means proactively seeking the necessary resources, information, and support to fulfill those expectations and succeed in your endeavors.

Overcoming Challenges: Resourcefulness is especially vital when faced with academic difficulties.

If you're struggling in classes, being resourceful means seeking available resources to prop yourself forward. This might involve utilizing tutoring services, seeking help from teachers or classmates, or exploring additional learning materials. Remember, those who access and use available resources are more likely to overcome challenges and achieve their goals.

Being resourceful is not about being on your own or reinventing the wheel. It's about recognizing the resources around you, asking for help when needed, and taking the initiative to find solutions. By cultivating this skill, you equip yourself with the tools to navigate life's complexities, overcome obstacles, and succeed. So, embrace your resourcefulness and let it guide you toward a future filled with possibilities.

My son, Hanif, was struggling with math. We all were frustrated. He refused to allow me to help him. Or were my methods flawed? Somehow, an argument or another trap interfered with the math tutoring attempts. I stopped trying to teach him math and focused on teaching him how to be resourceful enough to research the answers. There are dozens of tutorial sites online, some that I pointed out to him, and then later Hanif found out there were other resources like his own study-time management. And I was also resourceful. I hired a pretty 10th-grade student to be his tutor. My son did not present her with any of the resistance he had given me. In the end, simply teaching Hanif the math would not have had the impact that teaching him to be resourceful has had. The tutoring enhanced his math skills, and resourcefulness became a character trait.

Whenever I evaluate my involvement with Hanif's math dilemma, I can see areas of what some people call helicopter parenting, but not in large portions. I can understand the implications of helicopter parenting to the degrees of advantages and disadvantages, as listed in the next section. For example, had I not intervened, that would be the opposite of helicopter parenting, and we certainly would not choose that option.

Helicopter Parenting Can Limit Resourcefulness in Students

Let's talk about the oh-so-trendy topic of helicopter parenting. You know, that parenting style that makes you wonder if children are being raised or airlifted into adulthood. Brace yourselves as we navigate the choppy skies of the disadvantages and advantages of helicopter parenting – and maybe we'll even spot a few comedic co-pilots along the way.

Disadvantages of Helicopter Parenting:

Lack of Independence and Self-Reliance: Picture this: a child struggling to tie their shoelaces while Mom and Dad swoop in like superhero shoe-tying champions. Helicopter parenting can turn students into "Shoelace-Losers" who can't solve problems because they're used to parental rescue missions. It's like having a personal problem-solving butler!

Limited Opportunity for Decision-Making: Helicopter parents love to take the reins in decision-making. So, students, say goodbye to making choices and hello to a life of parental decree. Want cereal for breakfast? Tough luck; it's oatmeal! Who knew growing up was all about navigating a dictatorship?

Reduced Risk-Taking and Fear of Failure: With helicopter parents, failure is the enemy. Risk-taking? Nope, that's off the menu. Your offspring are so afraid of failing that they'd rather knit a safety net out of their bed sheets before attempting anything remotely daring. Creative solutions? No, they're just practicing their knitting.

Overdependence on External Support: Imagine a teenager faced with a science project question. Instead of tackling it head-on, they speed-dial their parents, grandparents, neighbors, and even the friendly mailman for help. Helicopter parenting can turn students into a one-person call center for problem-solving assistance.

Advantages of Helicopter Parenting:

Potential Benefits of Support and Guidance: Helicopter parents, for all their hovering, can be a fantastic support system. They're like a life coach on steroids, always there to guide you through life's obstacle course. Just be careful not to mistake them for GPS – they won't tell you where the nearest Starbucks is.

Striking a Balance is Advantageous: Helicopter parenting isn't all bad; it's just a matter of finding the right attitude. Striking a balance between letting students spread their wings and providing a soft landing when needed is like the Goldilocks of parenting – not too hot or cold, but just right.

In the end, folks, it's all about finding the perfect balance between letting students soar freely and giving them a little parental boost when the wind gets rough. After all, we want them to be resourceful enough to fix their problems but not so creative that they build a rocket ship in the backyard. Happy parenting, everyone, and remember, sometimes a little laughter is the best co-pilot on this crazy journey!

Tips for Parents and Teachers

In today's fast-paced and ever-changing world, being resourceful is a crucial skill for students to develop. It is a valuable skill that can empower students to navigate challenges, solve problems, and seize opportunities. Being resourceful goes beyond simply finding answers; it encompasses a mindset and a set of practices that foster creativity, collaboration, and critical thinking.

Resourcefulness is not just about finding answers; it is a mindset that fosters initiative, critical thinking, and problem-solving; it embraces curiosity, adaptability, and resilience. Help students understand that being resourceful involves having a positive attitude, being open to new ideas, and embracing challenges as opportunities for growth. Being resourceful empowers students to embrace failure as a stepping stone to success and explore alternative solutions. Foster a classroom environment encouraging students to take risks, think critically, and explore unconventional solutions.

Teach about the Resourceful Mindset: Resourcefulness starts with a mindset that sees challenges as opportunities for growth. A resourceful student understands that complex problems are inevitable and views them as puzzles waiting to be solved. By cultivating a mindset that values initiative, planning, organizing, and free thinking, students become better equipped to tackle obstacles and find innovative solutions.

Provide Opportunities for Students to Regularly Take the Initiative: Resourceful students take proactive steps to address problems rather than waiting for solutions to come to them. If they are not doing this, gently urge them by giving them small tasks first. When they demonstrate a sense of ownership over a small commission, praise them for actively seeking opportunities to learn, grow, and explore new avenues. For example, tell the student to find out where tutoring occurs at school or if it is even offered. Give no further instructions.

Create a safe space for students to reflect on their problem-solving experiences and openly discuss the outcomes.

Teach Embracing Failure as a Learning Opportunity: Encourage them to share their successful strategies and the challenges they faced. This open dialogue helps students learn from each other, gain insights into different perspectives, and understand that failures are valuable learning opportunities.

Provide Opportunities to Explore Alternative Options: Group projects can be a tremendous avenue for teaching resourcefulness in a classroom setting. This is especially true if a section of the project discusses how the group worked together, how they chose the final formats, and what other ideas group members had that were not explored. A lack of resourcefulness often stems from a limited perspective that restricts problem-solving to a single approach. Resourceful students, on the other hand, embrace the idea of exploring multiple options and thinking outside the box. They understand that there are often multiple paths to reach a solution and are willing to consider unconventional or innovative approaches.

Teach them to leverage technology, conduct research, seek expert guidance, and tap into their creativity. By exposing students to diverse problem-solving techniques, we empower them to overcome obstacles and develop a sense of self-reliance.

Celebrate When Students Devise Plans that Work Better Than the Plans of Baby Boomers:

Enough said. It has been rumored that some parents and teachers only allow one way of thinking… OUR way! L O L.

Teach Them to be Resolved: Give them a daily affirmation to chant. Let the assertion include thoughts like "Resourceful Students do not easily give up when faced with failure. Instead, they seek other solutions and approaches to achieve their goals. They exhibit resilience and determination, refusing to be disheartened by initial setbacks. They put in extra effort to explore other possibilities and find a way forward towards success."

Challenge the Student: Ask their opinion on how to do something or solve a problem. This is an excellent way to encourage them to be in charge of a volunteering exercise. One of the most effective ways to develop resourcefulness is through practical experience. Encourage students to take on leadership roles or volunteer to be in charge of a project or event because by assuming responsibilities and planning for a group, students will inevitably encounter issues that require problem-solving. This hands-on experience allows them to exercise their thought processes and develop their resourcefulness.

Emphasize the Power of Asking: "You don't get what you don't ask for." Encourage students to be proactive in seeking help, guidance, and resources. Teach them the value of asking questions, seeking clarification, and tapping into available support systems. By instilling confidence in students to seek assistance, you empower them to overcome challenges and access the resources they need to succeed.

Focus on Purpose: Our goal is to encourage resourcefulness and help students comprehend the purpose of their tasks and assignments. Connect their learning to real-world relevance and encourage them to think beyond the immediate requirements. When students grasp the bigger picture and recognize how their efforts contribute to a broader goal, it fuels their creativity and motivates them to explore possibilities beyond the obvious.

Being goal-directed involves setting objectives and working towards them, even in adversity. Teaching students the value of perseverance and resilience fosters their ability to stay motivated and determined when confronted with setbacks or obstacles. Resourceful individuals understand that setbacks are opportunities for growth and learning. They develop a resilient mindset that enables them to adapt, persevere, and ultimately achieve their goals.

Cultivating Time Management and Organization: Goal-directedness goes hand in hand with effective time management and organization skills. Resourceful individuals understand the importance of prioritizing tasks, setting deadlines, and managing time efficiently. We equip students with invaluable skills beyond academic settings by teaching them to set realistic goals, create action plans, and allocate their time effectively. These skills lay a foundation for success in various personal and professional endeavors.

When faced with a setback in a healthy environment, resourceful students can analyze their approach, learn from their mistakes, and adapt their strategies without fear. They understand that failure is not a definitive endpoint but a valuable lesson that guides them toward better solutions.

Teachers and parents must foster this atmosphere of acceptance of one's failures or setbacks. The household or classroom should be a safe environment where mistakes are discussed in the same manner as successes---to promote growth.

Resourcefulness Challenges for Introverted Students

Well, what about the shy, quiet introvert? I often meet parents who know their student is nervous, so they attempt to intervene on behalf of their student. In other words, they make the introductions as a parent to increase the likelihood that their scholar stands out.

That is one way to tackle it, but here is another, more personable manner. Students who are too shy to meet grownups or do not feel comfortable visiting their scholarship counselors should try writing letters. They could print it out if they typed it. They could put it in a sealed envelope addressed to the counselor (or teacher, or principal, etc.). With this simple method, this student has jumped to the front of the memory line. It would not have the same personal effect if they emailed an introduction.

You want to make yourself memorable, my friends!

CHAPTER 10: COLLEGE BOUND STUDENT-ATHLETES NEED TO HEAR THIS

Are we all clear that some parents deliberately hold their students back in elementary school or don't enroll them until they have to by law? One reason this might take place is sports-related. The purpose is to have a physically sound child to better compete in the athletic world. They hold their children back to ensure they are academically ready and give their students an edge above or raise them to other student-athletes. Whew! Now that we understand there is a continuum in the caliber of student-athletes and dozens of sports, from ESports to Flag Football, it should be equally clear how fuzzy things can be if students who wanted to participate after high school did not establish a plan of action.

At the high school level, there is typically an athletic director who is the point of contact for students with questions about competing at the next level. Coaches and school counselors also play a role in seeing student-athletes succeed. Unfortunately, these stakeholders may not communicate, and it is not always clear which athletes need special attention. For example, in 9th grade, a student may not know if she will play at the collegiate level and, therefore, may not plan for it.

There are several different college divisions.

College Athletic Divisions and Eligibility

NCAA, NAIA, and NJCAA Eligibility

With over 347 Division I schools, 312 Division II schools, more than 250 schools listed under NAIA, and over 100 JUCO opportunities, there are plenty of opportunities to participate in some division somewhere.

To participate in college sports, students must be registered with either the NCAA (National Collegiate Athletic Association) or NAIA (National Association of Intercollegiate Athletics). Alternatively, they can compete at the junior college (JUCO) level, governed by NJCAA (National Junior College Athletic Association). Many students transfer to a four-year university after completing two years at a JUCO, provided they meet the academic requirements.

The NAIA is another option for high school athletes interested in junior college-level sports. As stated, with 250 schools under its umbrella, NAIA offers various opportunities for athletic enthusiasts. While there are similarities between divisions, each one has its distinctive features.

Division III schools have the least strict conditions. Each NJCAA institution selects whether to compete at Division I, II, or III level for specific sports. Division I colleges can provide full athletic scholarships, which cover tuition, fees, room and board, course-related books, up to $250 in course-required supplies, and transportation costs to and from the college by the most direct route once per academic year. Division II colleges can only award tuition, fees, course-related books, and up to $250 in course-required supplies. Division III institutions cannot offer any athletically related financial assistance. However, NJCAA colleges that do not offer athletic aid can still choose to participate at the Division I or II level if they wish.

The NCAA has three division levels: Division I, II, and III.

A student is allowed to sign a Letter of Intent with both an NJCAA and an NCAA college without facing any consequences. However, signing an NJCAA Letter of Intent with two NJCAA colleges is prohibited. If a student does sign with two NJCAA colleges, they will be deemed ineligible to participate in any sport in the NJCAA competition for the following academic year. Once a student-athlete has signed an NJCAA Letter of Intent with an NJCAA member college, they will no longer be recruitable by any other NJCAA member college for the duration of the agreement.

The High School and the NCAA Clearinghouse

The NCAA evaluates a student's transcript for eligibility. Students should know before tenth grade which courses the NCAA will count to render a student eligible. Also of importance is students are not eligible to land paid for recruiting visits if they have not been cleared by the NCAA first. So, follow these steps:

1. Students are responsible for communicating their desire to participate in college-level athletics with the athletic director, coaches, and counselors.
2. Typically, college coaches send letters to schools when they are interested in a student-athlete. To be proactive, the student should find out who would receive their college offers and approach that person or office to determine how the letters will be distributed.
3. Students should create an account with the NCAA Clearinghouse at the end of their sophomore year.
4. Registering with the NCAA Clearinghouse costs around $85, but if students receive free or reduced lunch, they can request a fee waiver. Other financial issues could qualify them for this waiver.
5. Once the student starts the Clearinghouse application, they should request this waiver. Someone at the high school who is the designated Clearinghouse contact can then go in and approve the waiver application. Students can find out who that NCAA contact person is from their athletic director.
6. The eligibility center under "Resources" has a drop-down box with a link to approved courses. Access the "Brochure" and find the link for the approved courses under eligibilitycenter.org/courselist

Navigating Through the NCAA Clearinghouse

Signing up with the Clearinghouse is a simple process. Students must request their high school transcript to be sent and submit any required ACT or SAT scores. However, the NCAA has recently removed the ACT as a requirement. Additionally, they must watch a safety video related to sports and provide information about their sports involvement.

Sometimes, an athlete's height and body type may not meet the requirements of a particular sport or school in Division I. Students must review the baseline criteria for athletic and academic marks to understand where they stand compared to their dream school's rosters and future team members' stats. Setting realistic goals is crucial, and this should be done in the 8th or 9th grade. It's also important to note how versatile collegiate athletes are and develop that versatility early on. For instance, track and field sprinters must have more than one trick to be widely recruited. Competing in the 400-meter level or participating in jumps or hurdles in addition to sprints can increase their chances of being recruited.

While it may be challenging to double down on more than one sport in middle school, athletes can always fall back on a different sport to increase their options.

Promoting Yourself

It can be tempting to rely on others to handle everything, but student-athletes need to take control of their future. Successful athletes who receive scholarships proactively seek out coaches and contact colleges well before their junior year. They have a clear idea of where they want to attend college and play sports years before graduating from high school, but they take a closer look to determine how realistic their dream school really is. They have put together action videos, cleaned up their social media profile, drafted letters to coaches, and have them ready to send at the appropriate time.

Waiting until the junior or senior year to begin the research process is risky. It can put student-athletes at a disadvantage and could cause them to miss out on valuable opportunities. Student-athletes need to take charge of their future and start planning early.

One Egg and Ten Baskets

One of the main problems students face is starting the college application process too late and not being open-minded about their options. They might realize too late that taking a sure thing is better than gambling on something more significant. Some students might ignore opportunities to compete at smaller schools like NAIA or JUCO *because they know they qualify* and can aim for more meaningful opportunities. However, coaches might not see it that way, and other students with similar talent could already be on their radar. Not only that but there is great value in junior colleges.

CHAPTER 11: DIFFERENT TYPES OF SCHOOLS AND COLLEGES

Students who plan to attend trade schools, some colleges, or technical schools should be researching if the school is accredited or not. In this section, we will discuss the advantages and disadvantages of each, shedding light on the importance of making informed decisions.

Accredited and Non-Accredited Independent Schools

Accredited Schools:

a. Four-Year Universities: These institutions offer bachelor's degree programs across various disciplines and are known for their comprehensive curriculum, research opportunities, and campus life experience.

b. Two-Year Community Colleges: Community colleges provide associate degrees and certificate programs, offering a more affordable and accessible option for students pursuing higher education or gaining specific skills.

c. Technical Schools: These schools provide vocational training in specialized fields, such as automotive technology, culinary arts, or cosmetology.

d. Trade Schools: Trade schools offer targeted programs to develop practical skills in professions like real estate, dental hygiene, or HVAC (heating, ventilation, and air conditioning).

Non-Accredited Independent Schools: Independent schools not accredited by recognized accrediting bodies also exist. While they may offer valuable educational opportunities, students must exercise caution and thoroughly research such schools before enrolling.

Advantages and Disadvantages of Accredited and Non-Accredited Schools

Accredited Schools: Advantages:

Credibility and Quality Assurance: Accredited schools meet specific standards of educational quality, ensuring that students receive a recognized and respected education.

Access to Financial Aid: Accreditation is often a prerequisite for federal and state financial aid programs, making it easier for students to finance their education.

Transferability of Credits: Credits earned at accredited institutions are more likely to transfer to other colleges or universities if students pursue further education.

Accredited Schools Disadvantages:

Higher Costs: Four-year universities can be expensive, with tuition, room, board, and additional expenses. Students must consider their financial circumstances and weigh the cost against the potential benefits.

Rigorous Academics: Four-year universities often have demanding academic requirements, and students should assess their readiness for academic challenges before committing to such institutions.

Non-Accredited Independent Schools: Advantages and Disadvantages:

Focused Training: Non-accredited schools may offer specialized training programs in specific trades, providing students with practical skills for immediate employment opportunities.

Flexibility and Personalized Approach: These schools may provide more tailored curricula and smaller classes, allowing individualized attention and a more hands-on learning experience.

Disadvantages:

Lack of Accreditation: Non-accredited schools may not meet the established standards for educational quality and may not be recognized by employers or other educational institutions.

Limited Financial Aid Options: Students attending non-accredited schools are generally not eligible for federal or state financial aid programs, making it crucial to consider such institutions' financial implications and affordability.

Historically Black Colleges and Universities (HBCUs)

Historically Black Colleges and Universities (HBCUs) have played a crucial role in providing education and opportunities for so-called African-American students. While attending HBCUs has advantages and disadvantages, it is essential to recognize the significant contributions and successes associated with these institutions.

Advantages of Attending HBCUs:

1. Nurturing Environment: HBCUs often provide a supportive and inclusive environment that fosters community and belonging, as students share similar cultural experiences and backgrounds.
2. Cultural and Historical Relevance: HBCUs offer a unique educational experience by integrating Black history, culture, and traditions into their curricula, providing students with a comprehensive understanding of their heritage.
3. Strong Alumni Network: HBCUs have a strong alum network often dedicated to supporting and mentoring current students, which can lead to valuable connections and career opportunities.
4. Access to Role Models: Attending an HBCU exposes students to successful African-American professionals who serve as role models and inspire them to achieve their goals.

Disadvantages of Attending HBCUs:

Unfortunately, when a few HBCUs have poor client services, it gives a bad look for all HBCUs, and that is not true. Each HBCU is different.

1. Financial Constraints: HBCUs often face economic challenges and may have limited resources compared to some non-HBCUs. This can impact facilities, faculty salaries, research funding, and scholarship opportunities.
2. Limited Diversity: HBCUs predominantly serve African-American students, which

can result in a less diverse student body compared to other institutions.

3. Perceived Reputation: Despite the notable achievements and contributions of HBCUs, they may sometimes face stereotypes or a perceived lack of prestige compared to more well-known and established universities.

4. Long Waits on Applications and Return Phone Calls. However, this is not a fair assessment of all HBCUs at all.

It is important to note that these advantages and disadvantages may vary among different HBCUs, and individual experiences can differ significantly. Ultimately, choosing an educational institution should be based on personal preferences, academic goals, financial considerations, and the overall fit with a student's aspirations and values. HBCUs have proven influential in producing successful graduates and contributing to the African-American community and society.

A Few Famous People Who Attended HBCUs:

- Al Green, Reverend -Howard, Texas Southern, and Tuskegee University
- Alice Walker – Spelman College
- Bakari Sellers – Morehouse College
- Booker T. Washington -Hampton University
- DJ Envy (Raashaun Casey)– Hampton University
- Jesse Jackson, Reverend – North Carolina A&T
- Kamala Harris - Howard University
- Katherine Johnson – West Virginia State University
- Kenya Barris – Clark Atlanta University
- Langston Hughes – Lincoln University
- Louis Farrakhan, The Honorable Minister – Attended Winston-Salem University (Completed three years)
- Martin Luther King Jr. - Morehouse College
- Nikki Giovanni -Fisk University
- Oprah Winfrey - Tennessee State University
- Ralph David Abernathy – Alabama State University
- Ralph Ellison – Tuskegee University
- Samuel Jackson -Morehouse College
- Taraji Henson -Howard University
- Thurgood Marshall - Lincoln University (HBCU at the time) and Howard University
- Toni Morrison - Howard University
- Spike Lee - Morehouse College
- Stacey Abrams – Spelman College
- Stephen A. Smith – Winston-Salem University
- Wanda Sykes – Hampton University
- Yolanda Adams – Tennessee State University

CHAPTER 12: DEGREE TYPES

Associate Degree

An associate degree is an undergraduate academic degree students can pursue after completing high school or its equivalent. Community colleges, technical colleges, and some universities typically offer it. An associate degree is designed to provide a foundation of knowledge and skills in a specific field of study or prepare students for entry-level employment.

Here are some key points to understand about associate degrees and their benefits:

1. **Duration and Requirements:** Associate degree programs usually take two years of full-time study. They require the completion of a set number of credits or courses, which can vary depending on the program and institution.
2. **Specializations**: Associate degrees are available in a wide range of fields, including but not limited to business, healthcare, information technology, criminal justice, culinary arts, and early childhood education. These degrees are often more focused and career-oriented than bachelor's degrees' broader academic focus.
3. **Entry-Level Employment**: One of the primary benefits of earning an associate degree is that it can qualify you for entry-level positions in various industries. It provides practical skills and knowledge relevant to specific professions, which can give students an advantage when seeking employment after graduation.
4. **Cost-Effectiveness:** Associate degree programs are generally more affordable than bachelor's degree programs. They can be a cost-effective option for students who want to start their careers sooner or save money by completing the first two years of a four-year bachelor's degree at a community college before transferring to a university.
5. **Transfer Opportunities:** Many associate degree programs are designed to allow for easy transfer to a bachelor's degree program at a four-year university. This pathway is known as "transfer articulation" or "transfer agreements." It enables students to complete their general education requirements and foundational coursework at a community college before transferring to a university to complete their bachelor's degree.
6. **Career Advancement:** While an associate degree can lead to entry-level positions, some industries and professions may require a higher level of education for career advancement. In such cases, associate degree holders can use their degree as a stepping stone and continue their education by pursuing a bachelor's degree or higher.

In summary, an associate degree is an undergraduate degree that can be completed in two years. It provides specialized knowledge and skills in a specific field, prepares students for entry-level employment, and can serve as a cost-effective pathway to further education. Associate degrees are ideal for students who wish to start their careers sooner, gain practical skills, or eventually transfer to a four-year university to pursue a Bachelor's degree.

Bachelor's Degree

A bachelor's degree is an undergraduate academic degree students can pursue after completing high school or its equivalent. It provides a foundation in a specific field of study and is typically the first level of higher education.

Bachelor of Science (B.S.) and Bachelor of Arts (B.A.) are two common types of bachelor's degrees. Their main difference lies in the subjects they focus on and the approach they take in their coursework.

Bachelor of Science (B.S.): This degree is usually awarded in fields related to natural sciences, mathematics, engineering, technology, and some social sciences. It emphasizes a more scientific and technical approach to the subject matter. Students interested in biology, chemistry, physics, computer science, mathematics, or engineering might pursue a B.S. degree in those fields. B.S. programs often involve laboratory work, data analysis, problem-solving, and a focus on empirical evidence and quantitative methods.

Bachelor of Arts (B.A.): This degree is commonly awarded in fields related to humanities, social sciences, fine arts, languages, and liberal arts. It emphasizes a broader and more liberal education, focusing on literature, history, philosophy, sociology, psychology, or political science. B.A. programs often involve critical thinking, analysis of texts and ideas, research papers, and a focus on qualitative methods.

The distinction between B.S. and B.A. degrees can vary depending on the program and institution. Some fields may predominantly offer one type of degree, while others may offer both options. It's essential to consider your interests, strengths, and career goals when choosing between a B.S. and a B.A. degree.

It's worth noting that the difference in terminology can vary across countries and institutions. In some places, the distinction may not be explicitly mentioned, and all Bachelor's degrees may be referred to as a "Bachelor of Arts" degree.

In summary, a Bachelor's degree is the first level of higher education. A Bachelor of Science (B.S.) focuses on natural sciences, mathematics, and technical subjects, while a Bachelor of Arts (B.A.) emphasizes humanities, social sciences, and a broader liberal education.

Master's Degree

A master's degree is a postgraduate academic degree you can pursue after completing a bachelor's degree. It allows you to specialize in a particular field of study or area of professional practice and gain advanced knowledge and skills in that area.

There are two common types of master's degrees: Master of Arts (M.A.) and Master of Science (M.S.). Their main difference lies in the subjects they focus on and the approach they take in their coursework.

Master of Arts (M.A.): This degree is typically awarded in fields related to humanities, social sciences, and liberal arts. It emphasizes theoretical knowledge, critical thinking, and research skills. If you're interested in subjects like literature, history, sociology, psychology, or philosophy, you might pursue an M.A. degree in those fields. M.A. programs often involve extensive reading, research papers, and discussions to deepen your understanding of the subject.

Master of Science (M.S.): This degree is commonly awarded in fields related to natural sciences, engineering, technology, mathematics, and some social sciences. It focuses more on scientific and technical aspects, practical skills, and empirical research. If you are interested in computer science, biology, chemistry, physics, engineering, or economics, you might pursue an M.S. degree in those fields. M.S. programs often involve laboratory work, data analysis, experiments, and projects to apply theoretical concepts in real-world scenarios.

It's important to note that the division between M.A. and M.S. can vary depending on the specific program and institution. Some fields may offer both M.A. and M.S. degrees, while others may predominantly offer one type. The key is to choose a degree that aligns with your interests and future career goals.

In summary, a master's degree is a higher level of education that allows you to specialize in a specific field. A Master of Arts (M.A.) focuses on humanities and social sciences, emphasizing theoretical knowledge and research skills. A Master of Science (M.S.) emphasizes natural sciences, technology, and practical skills.

Doctor of Philosophy

What is a Doctor of Philosophy (Ph.D.)?

Imagine this as a quest for knowledge, with the ultimate treasure being a Ph.D. degree!

A Doctor of Philosophy, or Ph.D. for short, is the highest academic degree one can earn in many fields of study. Contrary to the name, it's not just about philosophy; it covers various subjects, from science and engineering to arts and humanities. The main focus of a Ph.D. program is research and contributing new knowledge to a chosen field.

The Ph.D. Journey:

Coursework: The Ph.D. adventure begins with rigorous coursework, where students study their field's foundations and current state of knowledge.

Research: The heart of a Ph.D. is original research. Students dive deep into a specific topic, conduct experiments, gather data, or analyze existing information to answer a research question or solve a problem.

Dissertation: Research findings are compiled into a lengthy dissertation document. This is the student's magnum opus, showcasing their expertise and contribution to the field.

Defense: Before a student is awarded a Ph.D., they must defend their dissertation before a panel of experts. It's like the final boss battle but with PowerPoint presentations instead of swords.

Jobs that Require or Benefit from a Ph.D.:

University Professor: Ph.D. holders often become university professors. They teach, conduct research, and mentor students in their field.

Research Scientist: In fields like biology, physics, or social sciences, a Ph.D. is essential for research positions. You might work in a lab, conduct experiments, and publish your findings.

Medical Doctor (MD/Ph.D.): Some doctors pursue a Ph.D. alongside their medical degree to engage in medical research or teach at medical schools.

Data Scientist/Analyst: Ph.D. holders in computer science or statistics are in demand for analyzing complex data and solving real-world problems.

Policy Analyst: In government or think tanks, Ph.D. holders analyze and develop policies, often in economics, public health, or environmental science.

Consultant: Management consultants with Ph. D.s might offer specialized expertise in various industries, from business to healthcare.

Archaeologist/Anthropologist: Ph.D. holders in these fields excavate ancient civilizations, study cultures, and contribute to our understanding of human history.

Psychologist: Clinical psychologists often hold a Ph.D. and help individuals with mental health issues through therapy and research.

Astronomer/Astrophysicist: Ph.D. astronomers study celestial objects and phenomena, while astrophysicists delve into the universe's physics.

Environmental Scientist: Ph.D. holders in this field research and develop solutions for environmental issues like climate change and conservation.

In summary, a Ph.D. is like obtaining the key to the treasure chest of specialized knowledge in a specialized field. It opens doors to various career paths, from academia and research to industry and policymaking. It's a challenging journey but a quest worth embarking on for those passionate about their subject and craving a more profound understanding.

Juris Doctorate

A Juris Doctorate (J.D.) is a professional degree required to become a lawyer in the United States. It is typically pursued after completing a bachelor's degree.

During law school, students study various aspects of the law, such as constitutional law, contracts, criminal law, and more. Students learn how the legal system works, how to analyze and apply rules to different situations, and how to argue cases in court.

The Juris Doctorate program typically takes three years to complete. It's an intense and challenging study period, but it's also rewarding because students gain a deep understanding of the law and the skills necessary to become a lawyer.

After earning the Juris Doctorate, students still need to pass the bar exam, which is an exam that tests their knowledge of the law. Passing the bar exam is necessary to obtain a license to practice law in a specific state.

Medical Doctor (M.D.)

An M.D. stands for Doctor of Medicine, and it is a professional degree that is required to become a medical doctor. It is the degree that qualifies individuals to practice medicine and treat patients.

Here are some essential points for high school students who are considering pursuing an M.D. degree:

Educational Journey: Becoming a medical doctor requires significant academic commitment. After high school, aspiring doctors typically need a bachelor's degree, which usually takes four years. Students must focus on pre-medical coursework during their undergraduate studies, including biology, chemistry, physics, and mathematics. Maintaining a high GPA and gaining relevant experience, such as volunteering at hospitals or clinics, can also strengthen their application to medical school.

Medical School: Students must apply to medical school after completing their bachelor's degree. Medical schools are highly competitive, and admission is based on factors such as GPA, Medical College Admission Test (MCAT) scores, letters of recommendation, personal statements, and interviews. Once accepted into medical school, students typically complete four years of intensive education and training.

Medical Curriculum: The medical school curriculum is designed to provide a comprehensive understanding of the human body, diseases, diagnosis, and treatment. Students learn various subjects, including anatomy, physiology, biochemistry, pharmacology, and pathology. They also receive clinical training through rotations in different medical specialties, gaining hands-on experience under the guidance of experienced physicians.

Residency Training: Aspiring doctors enter a residency program after graduating from medical school. Residency is a period of specialized training in a specific medical specialty, such as internal medicine, surgery, pediatrics, psychiatry, or obstetrics and gynecology. Residency programs can vary in duration, usually three to seven years, depending on the chosen specialty. During this time, residents work in hospitals, clinics, or other healthcare settings under the supervision of senior physicians.

Licensure and Specialization: Doctors must obtain a medical license to practice medicine independently after residency training. This typically involves passing a licensing exam specific to the country or state where they wish to practice. Additionally, doctors may pursue further specialization through fellowships, which provide advanced training in a particular area of medicine, such as cardiology, neurology, or dermatology.

CHAPTER 13: STEM FIELDS VERSUS LIBERAL ARTS

STEM Fields

When considering the pros and cons of majoring in a STEM field (Science, Technology, Engineering, Math) versus a Liberal Arts degree, it's important to note the extraordinary benefits that STEM fields offer:

High Demand and Job Security: STEM fields are known for their high demand and job security. With rapid advancements in technology and scientific research, there is a growing need for professionals with STEM expertise. This translates into more excellent job opportunities and long-term career stability.

Competitive Salaries: STEM careers often have higher earning potential than liberal arts. The demand for specialized skills and the scarcity of qualified professionals contribute to competitive salaries in STEM occupations.

Technological Advancements and Innovation: STEM fields drive technological advancements and innovation, shaping our world. By pursuing a STEM degree, students can actively contribute to groundbreaking discoveries, solve complex problems, and positively impact society.

Problem-Solving and Analytical Skills: STEM education cultivates strong problem-solving and analytical skills. These critical thinking abilities are highly valued in various professional settings and can be applied to diverse challenges beyond the field of study.

Interdisciplinary Collaboration: STEM fields often require interdisciplinary collaboration, fostering teamwork and communication skills. Working with professionals from different backgrounds and expertise promotes a diverse and enriching work environment.

Financial Considerations: Regarding financial considerations, the potential for higher salaries in STEM fields can contribute to better financial stability and future earning potential. This can include higher starting salaries, opportunities for career advancement, and potential for increased earnings over time.

Global Relevance: STEM fields have a worldwide impact and are highly relevant in addressing pressing global challenges. From climate change to healthcare advancements, STEM professionals are crucial in finding solutions that impact societies worldwide.

Innovation and Entrepreneurship: STEM fields often foster a culture of innovation and entrepreneurship. The skills and knowledge gained in STEM disciplines can empower individuals to start businesses, create groundbreaking technologies, and contribute to economic growth and development.

Transferable Skills: While STEM fields have specific technical skills, they also equip students with valuable transferable skills across various industries. These include problem-solving, data analysis, critical thinking, and adaptability. Such skills can be applied to multiple career paths, offering flexibility and resilience in a rapidly changing job market.

Addressing Future Workforce Needs: The world increasingly relies on technology and scientific advancements. By pursuing STEM fields, students position themselves at the forefront of emerging industries and are more likely to meet future workforce demands.

Collaboration with Liberal Arts: The intersection of STEM and liberal arts can lead to powerful outcomes. Integrating humanities, social sciences, and skills with STEM disciplines fosters well-rounded professionals who can approach complex problems holistically, combining technical expertise with ethical considerations and humanistic perspectives.

Women and African Americans in STEM Fields

There's a shortage of women and African Americans in STEM fields, and you care because whenever there is a high need, more benefits become available. Encouraging diversity and inclusion in STEM is a matter of social justice and an economic imperative. Increasing representation of underrepresented groups in STEM leads to diverse perspectives, innovative solutions, and a more robust workforce overall. Efforts to bridge the gender and racial gaps in STEM involve promoting STEM education early, providing mentorship and support networks, and addressing systemic barriers that hinder access and opportunities for marginalized groups.

Liberal Arts Education

For liberal arts degrees, it's essential to highlight the intrinsic value they offer. Liberal arts education promotes critical thinking, effective communication, cultural understanding, and a broader societal perspective. These skills are highly sought after by employers who recognize the importance of well-rounded professionals capable of adapting to a dynamic workplace.

While STEM fields offer remarkable benefits, it is essential to recognize the value of a liberal arts degree as well. Liberal arts education emphasizes critical thinking, creativity, communication skills, and a well-rounded world understanding. It can provide a strong foundation for adaptability, empathy, and a broader perspective.

However, it is worth noting that majoring in a liberal arts area may have some financial considerations and perceived risks. Some of these concerns include potentially lower starting salaries, a more competitive job market in specific fields, and a perceived mismatch between the skills acquired and specific job opportunities.

In conclusion, both STEM and liberal arts degrees have their unique benefits and considerations. While STEM fields offer extraordinary prospects regarding job demand, salaries, and innovation, it is essential to recognize the value of a liberal arts education in fostering critical thinking, creativity, and a well-rounded perspective. Promoting diversity in STEM, including addressing the shortage of women and African Americans, is vital for creating a more inclusive and equitable future. Ultimately, students should choose a field of study that aligns with their passions, interests, and long-term goals.

CHAPTER 14: COLLEGE AFFORDABILITY AND LOANS

College Affordability

Different schools offer different amounts of help to pay for college. Things like good grades, financial need, where the school is, and whether it's public or private can affect how affordable a college is for you. Free college money comes in grants, gifts, scholarships, and interest earned if the student is assigned to a college savings plan. Grants are typically awarded based on financial need, as determined by the information on the Free Application for Federal Student Aid (FAFSA) or other financial aid forms. Some grants, like Pell Grants, are specifically need-based.

A good number of students want scholarships to pay for college. However, taking out a student loan is the reality for around 40% of college students. Choosing suitable loans and understanding how they work is important. It's also essential to consider how much college will cost and what kind of help you can get from the school.

Ideas to Pay for College

Apply for Additional Scholarships: Numerous scholarships are available for students facing financial difficulties or unique circumstances. Research and apply for scholarships that align with your background, interests, and academic achievements. Reach out to community organizations, local businesses, and foundations that offer scholarships in your area.

Explore Federal Student Aid: Complete the Free Application for Federal Student Aid (FAFSA) to determine your eligibility for federal grants, work-study programs, and low-interest student loans. The FAFSA considers each family's financial situation and aids based on their demonstrated need.

Seek Institutional Aid: Students should contact the financial aid offices at their accepted colleges and explain their situation. They may have additional resources or institutional scholarships to support students facing financial hardships.

Consider Work-Study Programs: Many colleges offer work-study programs where students can work part-time on campus to earn money to cover their educational expenses. These positions often align with the student's field of study and provide valuable work experience.

Research Tuition Payment Plans: Inquire about flexible tuition payment plans the colleges offer. These plans allow students to pay their tuition and fees in installments over the semester, making it more manageable for their financial situation.

Explore Community College Transfer Options: If affording a four-year college immediately seems challenging, consider starting at a community college. Community colleges often have lower tuition costs, and students can take advantage of transfer programs to eventually transfer to a four-year college or university.

Seek Part-Time Employment: Students should look for part-time job opportunities in their community to help cover their living expenses or save for college. Balancing work and studies can be challenging, but it can provide students with valuable financial support.

Utilize Crowdfunding Platforms: Consider setting up a crowdfunding campaign to raise funds for college education. Students can share their stories, aspirations, and financial needs with family, friends, and the community.

Investigate Non-Traditional Scholarships: Consider unconventional scholarships or grants specific to the intended major, extracurricular activities, or personal background. There are scholarships available for various talents, hobbies, or unique experiences.

Seek Guidance from Nonprofit Organizations: Reach out to nonprofit organizations that help students from low-income families or those facing challenging circumstances. These organizations may offer financial aid, mentorship programs, or resources to support your educational journey.

Understanding Student Loans: Federal vs. Private

Federal Loans:

1. These loans come from the U.S. Department of Education.
2. There are three types: Subsidized, Unsubsidized, and PLUS loans.
3. Subsidized loans are for students who show they need financial help. They don't charge interest until you're done with school.
4. Unsubsidized loans are for everyone, but they charge interest immediately (you can delay payments until six months after graduating).
5. PLUS loans are for graduate students and parents with no set borrowing limit.

Benefits of Federal Loans:

1. Lower fixed interest rates compared to private loans.
2. Various payment options, loan forgiveness, and protection programs.
3. Payments start six months after leaving school.
4. No need for a credit history.
5. It takes a while to default if you can't make payments.

Downsides of Federal Loans:

1. Some are based on financial "need" and might not cover all your expenses.
2. There's a limit on how much you can borrow.
3. Parents or guardians must complete the FAFSA with you.
4. Private Student Loans:
5. Banks, credit unions, and other lenders offer these loans.
6. Interest rates and amounts vary based on your credit history, income, and co-signer.

Benefits of Private Loans:

1. You can use them to cover school costs after other options are exhausted.

2.   You can borrow more (up to 100% of your school costs).

3.   They can improve your credit score.

4.   There's a time limit (3 to 10 years) if you can't pay.

5.   International students can get them.

Downsides of Private Loans:

1.   Fewer options for repayment plans and protection.

2.   Higher interest rates, which might change.

3.   You might need a co-signer.

Student Loan Amortization:

This is about paying off your debt monthly, including the amount you borrowed (principal) and extra money (interest).

Over time, you pay more toward what you borrowed and less for interest.

You can save money by paying more each month if you can.

CHAPTER 15: EVERYTHING YOU NEED TO KNOW ABOUT SCHOLARSHIPS

Dear Students, this chapter is essential for your scholarship journey, but please note that the previous chapters provide crucial base knowledge.

Stacking Scholarships

Scholarships are typically monetary gifts to be used toward education that you do not have to repay. Scholarships include books, supplies, tuition, room and board, and other school-related fees. Scholarships never have to be paid back, unlike loans. Scholarships must be reported to the financial aid department at the college. Some schools allow students to stack scholarships, while others do not. Stacking scholarships means receiving more than one scholarship and stacking or adding them together. However, the financial aid department at the college is the person who gets the scholarship on your behalf. If they have a "non-stacking" agenda, they will subtract outside scholarships from the total due before applying for internal awards. This means you could potentially receive less overall. If scholarships are stacked and if there is access to scholarship money, the student could get that back as a refund.

Completing Scholarship Applications

Online Scholarships -Available through online platforms or websites that connect students with various opportunities. Completing scholarships typically occurs online, and students answer all the questions and upload documents like essays, transcripts -or transcripts may have to be sent separately by an online service like Parchment.

Paper-Pencil Scholarships -Great scholarships with a lower applicant pool.

Completing scholarships typically occurs online, and students answer all the questions and upload documents like essays, transcripts -or transcripts may have to be sent separately by an online transcript service that your school uses. Required letters of recommendation must usually be sent to the scholarship committee directly by the recommender, not the student.

Different Types of Scholarships

Academic Scholarships: Awarded based on academic achievement, such as high GPA, standardized test scores (SAT, ACT), and class ranking.

Athletic Scholarships: For exceptional athletes who excel in sports and plan to continue their athletic involvement in college.

Business or Industry Scholarships: Local businesses, companies, or industries sometimes offer scholarships to students pursuing specific fields or career paths. These scholarships can be tied to local industries, such as healthcare, technology, or agriculture. Advantages: Business or industry scholarships often have a more targeted applicant pool, making them less competitive than broader national scholarships. They may also provide networking opportunities or potential internships or job connections within the local industry.

Career-Specific Scholarships: Geared toward students planning to pursue specific careers, such as nursing, teaching, or engineering.

College or University Scholarships: Many colleges and universities have specific scholarships for local or regional students. These scholarships may be based on academic achievements, leadership qualities, or particular talents or skills. Advantages: College or university scholarships can provide financial support while attending a local institution. They are often designed to support local talent and encourage students to stay in the area, fostering community growth and development.

Community Service Scholarships: Awarded to students who commit to volunteering and community involvement.

Creative Arts Scholarships: For students with talents in visual arts, performing arts, creative writing, or filmmaking.

Essay Scholarships: Students must write on a specific topic or prompt to demonstrate their writing skills, critical thinking, and creativity.

Entrepreneurial Scholarships: For students who have demonstrated entrepreneurial spirit and plan to start their businesses.

First-Generation Scholarships: Awarded to students who are the first in their family to attend college.

Foundation Scholarships: Private foundations or nonprofit organizations provide scholarships to support education.

International Scholarships: Available for students who plan to study abroad or attend universities outside their home country.

Legacy Scholarships: Awarded to students with a family member (parent, grandparent, etc.) who attended a specific college or university.

Leadership Scholarships: Granted to students with exceptional leadership qualities and skills through school, extracurricular activities, or community involvement.

Local Scholarships: Students can tap into opportunities tailored to their community and individual circumstances by applying for local scholarships. These scholarships often have less competition than national awards, increasing the likelihood of receiving financial support. Additionally, local scholarships allow students to strengthen connections within their community, foster local support networks, and potentially gain exposure to internships or job opportunities.

Merit-Based Scholarships: Given to students with exceptional talents, skills, or accomplishments in areas like arts, music, athletics, or leadership.

Military Scholarships: Offered to students interested in joining the military or pursuing a career in the armed forces.

Minority Scholarships: Aimed at underrepresented minority groups to increase diversity and inclusion in higher education.

Need-Based Scholarships: Provided to students based on financial need, often determined by the Free Application for Federal Student Aid (FAFSA) or other financial aid forms.

Niche (Hobby or Interest) Scholarships: Granted to students with unique hobbies or interests, such as gaming, fashion, or gardening.

Philanthropic Foundation Scholarships: Local philanthropic foundations or trusts sometimes offer scholarships to students within their community. These foundations may have specific focuses, such as supporting underserved populations, promoting educational equity, or funding students pursuing specific majors. Advantages: Philanthropic foundation scholarships can align with your background, interests, or career goals. These scholarships often have a more personalized and localized application process, allowing you to showcase your unique qualities or experiences.

State and Local Scholarships: Offered by state governments, local organizations, or businesses to students from specific regions.

STEM Scholarships: Targeted at students interested in pursuing science, technology, engineering, or mathematics fields.

Fifty (50) Online Scholarship Search Engines

Many online scholarship search engines and databases can help you find scholarships based on your interests, background, and academic achievements. Some popular options include:

1. **Achieve Alabama -** Provides essential state-specific information that addresses the economic imperative, the equity imperative, and the expectations imperative of the college- and career-ready agenda. **[Link: https://www.achieve.org/alabama]**

2. **Alabama Scholarships -** Provides several resources to find scholarships based on location. **[Link:https://www.scholarships.com/financial-aid/college-scholarships/scholarships-by-state/alabama-scholarships/]**

3. **American Indian College Fund-** Provides Native American students with scholarships and financial support for 33 accredited tribal colleges and universities. **[Link:https://www.google.com/url?q=http://www.collegefund.org/&sa=D&source=editors&ust=1697215685316373&usg=AOvVaw3A-KVdCl2QveXBYmsNFcFj]**

4. **American Indian Graduate Center-** The largest scholarship provider to Native students in the United States, awarding $15 million in scholarships annually and more than $200 million since inception. For almost 50 years, AIGC has funded students pursuing undergraduate, graduate, and professional degrees in any field of study at any accredited institution of choice, working with over 500 tribes in all 50 states. **[Link:https://www.google.com/url?q=http://www.aigcs.org/&sa=D&source=editors&ust=1697216007335102&usg=AOvVaw3i2srM0tPzga_EE-7**

oyCcX]

5. **Asian and Pacific Islander American Scholarship Fund-** The nation's largest non-profit organization devoted to providing college scholarships for Asian Americans and Pacific Islanders (AAPI). [**Link:http://www.apiasf.org/scholarship_apiasf.html**]

6. **Cappex -** A free website to learn which colleges want you before you apply and about more than $11 billion in merit aid scholarships. [**Link: https://www.blackscholarships.org/2018/09/scholarships-available-beyonce-beygood-jay-z-shawn-carter-foundation.html**]

7. **Cash Course-** Information that helps college students stay financially informed. [**Link: http://cashcourse.org/**]

8. **Chegg-** A place to connect with scholarships and learn about colleges. [**Link: https://www.chegg.com/scholarships**]

9. **College Board-**We're a mission-driven not-for-profit organization that connects students to college success. [**Link: https://collegeboard.com/**]

10. **College Green Light-** Here to help students take control of their financial futures. No cost, no catch, no hidden agenda. [**Link: https://www.collegegreenlight.com/**]

11. **College Raptor-**Helping students find government, institutional, and private scholarships. [**Link: https://www.collegeraptor.com/2500scholarship/**]

12. **College Scholarships-** We have relationships with educational consultants, financial aid directors/officers, and others who work daily on a face-to-face basis with college students and their financial issues. [**Link: http://www.collegescholarships.org/scholarships/**]

13. **Common Knowledge Scholarship Foundation-** Educational and scholarship opportunities for students of all levels. [**Link: http://cksf.org/**]

14. **DAR Scholarships-** The scholarships range from general (no specific major), nursing, medicine, occupational or physical therapy, English, science, math, law, music, history, American Studies, chemistry, horticulture, elementary and secondary education, and business administration. [**Link: https://dar.academicworks.com/**]

15. **Dell Scholars program-** Recognizes academic potential and determination in students with a definite need for financial assistance. [**Link: http://www.dellscholars.org/**]

16. **Fast Web -** Create a profile and let Fastweb research scholarships, internships, colleges, and more for you. [**Link: https://www.fastweb.com/**]

17. **Flavorful Futures Scholarship-**Scholarships based on your strengths, interests, and skills. [**Link: Posted in college and career center**]

18. **Gates Millenium Scholars-**Provides outstanding low-income African American, American Indian/Alaska Native, Asian Pacific Islander American, and Hispanic American students with an opportunity to complete an undergraduate college education in any discipline they choose. [**Link: http://www.gmsp.org/**]

19. **Get Schooled-**Get Schooled helps young people get to college, find their first jobs, and succeed. [**Link: https://getschooled.com/dashboard**]

20. **Going Merry-** A free scholarship and financial aid platform with personalized matching of students to thousands of scholarships. [**Link:www.goingmerry.com**]

21. **Goizueta Legacy Scholarship-**Provides scholarships for the children of Coca-Cola employees. [**Link: Goizueta Legacy Scholarship**]

22. **GoodCall** - GoodCall is a scholarship search engine that helps students find available scholarships based on their personal information and interests. It offers a vast database of scholarship opportunities to assist students in funding their education. [Link: **https://www.goodcall.com/scholarships/**]

23. **Hispanic Scholarship-** The HSF Scholarship is designed to assist students of Hispanic heritage in obtaining a university degree. Scholarships are available on a competitive basis. [**Link: https://hsf.net/en/scholarships/programs/general-college-scholarships**]

24. **HS Finder (Hispanic Scholarship Fund)-** Scholarship information for Latino students. [**Link: HS Finder (Hispanic Scholarship Fund)**]

25. **JLV College Counseling-** Where you can find any scholarships from ethnicity to gender. [**Link: https://jlvcollegecounseling.com/scholarships/**]

26. **JROTC and Beyond Scholarships-**Scholarships for rising high school juniors at both Freedoms Foundation – Valley Forge and many regional sites nationwide in partnership with the Military Order of World Wars. [**Link: https://www.nationalsojourners.org/youth-leadership-programs/#essay**]

27. **Know How 2G-**Complete information on college prep, whether in middle school or seniors. [**Link: knowhow2go.org**]

28. **Kuder-**Unlock a world of possibilities with the Alabama Career Planning System! Explore careers, find college matches, build education plans, create shareable portfolios, and more – all guided by personalized career interests, skills, confidence, and work values. [**Link: https://al.kuder.com**]

29. **NSHSS Foundation-**The NSHSS Foundation fosters the growth of students pursuing the STEAM (science, technology, engineering, arts, and math), business, economics, public policy, and environmental science and sustainability fields. Through special programs, including the NSHSS Honor Society, the NSHSS Foundation connects young scholars with additional opportunities to advance their education, personal growth, and career interests. [**Link: https://nshssfoundation.org/**]

30. **Peerlift-** Proven scholarships, internships, summer programs, and more gathered by fellow students like you. [**Link: peerlift.org**]

31. **Peterson's Scholarship Search-** Peterson's is a comprehensive college and career information resource. It offers college search tools, test preparation resources, scholarship databases, and financial aid and admissions guidance. [**Link: https://www.petersons.com/**]

32. **Potential Magazine** - Archives of several different in and out-of-state scholarships. [**Link: http://potentialmagazine.com/topics/college-scholarships/**]

33. **Raise Me -** Add grades, sports, and other achievements, and receive micro-scholarships for each achievement. They will be rewarded once you are in attendance

at that college. [Link: https://www.raise.me/]

34. **Reagan Foundation Scholarships** - Scholarship opportunities for outstanding student leaders. [Link: https://www.reaganfoundation.org/education/scholarship-programs/]

35. **Scholar Snapp** - A free, simple-to-use data standard that allows students to reuse their application information - including contact information, essays, transcripts, etc. - from one scholarship application to another, streamlining the college application process. [Link: http://www.scholarsnapp.org/]

36. **Scholarship America** - Provides information and resources for your scholarship search. [Link: http://scholarshipamerica.org/]

37. **Scholarship Buddy** - Provides scholarship information to high school and college students in the United States. [Link: https://scholarshipbuddy.com/scholarships]

38. **Scholarship.com** - Scholarship.com is a popular scholarship search engine that helps students find scholarships based on their profile and qualifications. It provides a wide range of scholarship opportunities from various sources. [Link: https://www.scholarships.com/]

39. **Scholly** - A mobile app that provides students a fast and straightforward way to find college scholarships. [Link: https://myscholly.com/]

40. **Student Scholarships** - Links to many resources- new scholarships, popular scholarships, course outlines, careers and salaries, etc. [Link: http://www.studentscholarships.org/]

41. **Students with Disabilities Scholarships** - Links to several unique scholarship opportunities for students with disabilities. [Link: http://www.collegescholarships.org/disabilities.htm]

42. **Strive Forward** - Strive Forward offers a scholarship and financial literacy program available to graduating seniors in the Huntsville City, Madison City, and Madison County school districts. Our programs are designed to assist graduating seniors in accomplishing their educational goals while equipping them to make sound financial decisions as they transition into adulthood. [Link: https://www.striveforward.net/]

43. **Student-View Scholarship Program** - "An amazing program that serves as a resource for both colleges and students –offering information to colleges and opportunities to students." [Link: http://www.student-view.com/]

44. **The American Legion** - Several merit-based scholarships, including those geared towards the children of veterans. [Link: https://www.legion.org/scholarships]

45. **Thurgood Marshall College Fund** - Provides scholarships, programmatic and capacity-building support to the 47 public Historically Black Colleges and Universities (HBCUs). [Link: http://www.thurgoodmarshallfund.net/]

46. **Tuition Funding Services (TFS)** - [Link: https://www.tuitionfundingsources.com/]

47. **UNCF** - Awards 10,000 students each year through 400 scholarship and

internship programs so that students from low- and moderate-income families can afford college tuition, books, and room and board. [**Link: http://www.uncf.org/**]

48.	**Excellence In Process Industrial Controls (EPIC) -** The Excellence in Process Industrial Controls program at Calhoun Community College combines an Associate of Applied Science degree in Process Technology with two years of paid, related co-op work experience with a sponsor company. Students accepted in this competitive program typically attend school.[**Link: http://calhoun.edu/EPIC**]

49.	**Strive Forward-** Strive Forward offers a scholarship and financial literacy program available to graduating seniors in the Huntsville City, Madison City, and Madison County school districts. Our programs are designed to assist graduating seniors in accomplishing their educational goals while equipping them to make sound financial decisions as they transition into adulthood.[**Link: https://www.striveforward.net/**]

50.	**Tuition Funding Services (TFS)-** @tuitionfundingsources.com[**Link: https://www.tuitionfundingsources.com/**]

Where Else to Find Scholarships

Finding scholarships can be a bit of a process, but there are several effective methods that students can use to locate the types of scholarships mentioned earlier:

High School Guidance Counselors: Start by speaking with your school's guidance counselor. They often have information about local scholarships and can guide where to look for other opportunities.

College and University Websites: Check the websites of the colleges and universities you're interested in. They often offer scholarships specifically for their incoming students.

Community Organizations and Clubs: Many local community organizations and foundations offer scholarships. Examples include rotary clubs, Lions clubs, local chambers of commerce, and nonprofit organizations.

Professional Associations: If you're interested in a specific field or career path (such as engineering, nursing, or journalism), seek scholarships from relevant professional associations.

Company and Employer Scholarships: Some companies offer scholarships to employees' children or students pursuing careers related to their industry.

Public Libraries: Visit your local public library. They often have resources and information about scholarships available in your area.

Social Media and Online Groups: Follow scholarship-related accounts on social media platforms and join online forums or groups dedicated to scholarship opportunities.

Financial Aid Offices: If you're already in contact with colleges or universities, their financial aid offices can provide information about scholarships available to their students.

Local Newspapers and News Stations: Watch local media outlets for announcements about scholarships and educational opportunities.

Ask Teachers and Mentors: Your teachers, coaches, mentors, and community leaders might know of scholarship opportunities or be able to provide guidance.

Niche Websites: For specific interests like art, music, or sports, look for websites or organizations dedicated to those areas that offer scholarships.

Online Forums and Communities: Participate in online forums or communities where students discuss scholarship opportunities and share advice.

Attend College Fairs and Workshops: Attend college fairs and workshops in your area to learn about scholarships and financial aid options.

Remember to keep track of application deadlines, requirements, and any necessary documentation. Creating a calendar or spreadsheet to stay organized and ensure you don't miss any opportunities is also a good idea.

29 Essential Tips about Scholarships

1. Read the fine print. Determine **why they are giving money away**. Are they earning more than they are giving because you signed an agreement stating they can sell your personal information to third parties? Is it a sweepstake where the student doesn't have to meet any requirements? Sweepstakes often involve collecting student data to sell to other companies. Students should weigh the odds of winning the sweepstakes against possibly being spammed exponentially.

2. Submit a complete application. You can multiply your chances of winning just by being thorough. Students miss out on scholarship monies repeatedly due to forgotten signatures, a missing portrait, or failure to complete all sections and mail supporting documents. Follow instructions diligently and ensure all required elements are included. Attention to detail is crucial when submitting scholarship applications. You present yourself as an organized and responsible candidate by following instructions meticulously and ensuring all required components are included.

3. Answer all application questions thoroughly: Provide comprehensive responses to showcase your qualifications. Providing thorough and well-thought-out responses to application questions allows scholarship committees to gain deeper insight into your qualifications, achievements, and aspirations.

4. Ask college recruiters. This is another reason students should visit their college and career center, a cesspool for recruiters. College recruiters either sit on scholarship boards, know someone on the board, or they make scholarship recommendations to the board.

5. Essay templates should be written in advance.

6. Take various standardized tests: Try the ACT and SAT to showcase different strengths. Take standardized tests: Standardized tests like the ACT and SAT play a vital role in scholarship applications, allowing you to showcase your academic abilities and increase your eligibility for a more comprehensive range of scholarships.

7. The ACT measures achievement, while the SAT measures aptitude.

Understanding the distinction between the ACT (achievement-based) and SAT (aptitude-based) helps you strategize and determine which test aligns better with your strengths, maximizing your scholarship prospects.

8. Prioritize early test-taking: Take the ACT as early as possible to allow for necessary retakes. Taking standardized tests early gives you more opportunities to improve your scores, ensuring you present your best possible performance to scholarship committees.

9. Diversify your scholarship search: Don't rely solely on standardized test scores. Relying exclusively on standardized test scores may limit your options. By diversifying your scholarship search, you open yourself to a broader range of opportunities, considering various aspects of your skills and achievements.

10. Polish your writing skills: Craft compelling essays highlighting your uniqueness. Your essay is a powerful tool for setting yourself apart from other applicants. Effective essays showcase your unique experiences, perspectives, and aspirations, making a solid impression on scholarship committees.

11. Start early with essay writing: Begin developing essays based on personal challenges or obstacles overcome. Beginning your essay writing process early allows you to create thoughtful narratives and refine your writing skills. This preparation leads to more compelling essays that captivate the attention of scholarship reviewers.

12. Have a couple of teachers read over your essay.

13. Reflect on volunteerism and community involvement: Showcase your contributions and creativity. Scholarship committees value your commitment to community service and volunteer work. Sharing your experiences and gifts highlights your character and demonstrates your dedication to making a positive impact.

14. Highlight skills developed through babysitting or other jobs: Emphasize trust, communication, and responsibilities. Highlight employment experiences, even if they seem unrelated to academics. Employment experiences can reveal valuable skills such as responsibility, communication, and trustworthiness. Emphasizing these skills shows scholarship committees your potential for growth and success.

15. Discuss household chores and helping family members: Demonstrate your willingness to contribute. Don't overlook the importance of responsibilities within your own home. Mentioning your duties or assistance to family members demonstrates your work ethic, dependability, and willingness to contribute.

16. Focus on likability and community placement: Showcase your positive impact and relationships. Being well-liked and respected within your community can set you apart as a valuable asset. Scholarship committees seek individuals who can positively influence their environment and make meaningful societal contributions.

17. Explain your financial need: Articulate why you require financial assistance for college. Articulating your financial condition is essential to scholarship applications, regardless of your family's income level. You demonstrate your

determination to pave your way and minimize debt by expressing your reasons for seeking financial assistance.

18. Consider family financial circumstances: Consult with parents or guardians to better understand the situation. Understanding your family's financial situation is crucial to accurately representing your financial needs. It helps you paint a comprehensive picture of your family's challenges and expenses, providing context for your scholarship application.

19. Discuss bills, expenses, and family health issues: Show the broader financial context affecting your family. By discussing bills, fees, and health issues that affect your family, you shed light on the financial burdens your family might be experiencing. This transparency enables scholarship committees to understand the complex realities impacting your educational journey.

20. Broaden your scholarship search: Apply for scholarships even if you don't perfectly match the criteria. Don't limit yourself to scholarships that match your qualifications exactly. Applying for scholarships you're close to qualifying for expands your opportunities, as fewer applicants for those awards may exist.

21. Pay attention to deadlines: Missing deadlines can disqualify your application, so be proactive and organized. Missing deadlines can be detrimental to your scholarship prospects. Staying on top of application timelines demonstrates your commitment and punctuality, traits highly valued by scholarship committees.

22. Send complete applications together: Adhering to application guidelines and submitting all required materials together showcases your ability to follow instructions and present a finished and polished application. Ensure all the necessary materials are offered as instructed.

23. Dedicate time for scholarship applications: Treat the process as a job and allocate sufficient time for research, preparation, and submission of the applications.

24. Stay organized: Utilize tools like Microsoft Excel or create your template to track scholarships, deadlines, and requirements. Utilize available templates: Access existing scholarship application templates to streamline your submissions.

25. Seek advice and guidance: Contact counselors, mentors, or scholarship advisors for assistance and support. Don't hesitate to contact counselors, mentors, or scholarship advisors for help and guidance. Their expertise can provide valuable insights and enhance your scholarship search.

26. Explore niche scholarships: Find scholarships that align with your interests, talents, or cultural background. Scholarships tailored to your specific interests, skills, or cultural experience provide excellent opportunities for recognition and financial aid. Researching and applying for these niche scholarships can significantly increase your chances of success.

27. Consider your heritage -are you Native American? Irish? Jewish? Left-handed? There are scholarships for almost everyone! Are you a cancer survivor? Do you have a sibling with Cancer? What about a parent who was a fallen hero? A war

veteran or a police officer?

28. Use your skills to apply, and not just your GPA.

29. Apply, apply, apply: Apply for as many scholarships as possible to increase your chances of receiving financial aid for college. Applying for as many scholarships as possible is crucial. By casting a wide net and submitting applications, even if you don't perfectly match the criteria, you increase your chances of receiving financial aid.

CHAPTER 16: ACT, SAT, AND OTHER STANDARDIZED TESTS

The Main Questions Students Have about the ACT

Harmony: What if the school requires a 25 on the ACT, but my score is only a 23? Should I apply? Even though the school is test-optional, the recruiter said my ACT score would be needed for scholarship consideration.

Dr. Muhammad: The answer is no; as long as the score you earned is high enough to aid in your admission, go ahead and apply. Sometimes, it could take a school several weeks to process an application. Getting admitted and *then resubmitting* test scores would be wiser if it benefits you after retaking the test.

You might be able to get into the school with a 23, but my guess is your ACT score would have to be raised significantly to qualify for merit scholarships at that school. The school could offer different types of scholarships that do not consider the ACT score. My second thought is to have you take the SAT. Schools usually will allow students to submit either test. Given that the SAT is an entirely different type of evaluation, students who do poorly on the ACT might do better on the SAT. By the way, a 23 score is pretty decent -about three points above the national average.

Seth: I feel bad for asking you this, but I can't access my ACT account to access my score to send to colleges.

Dr. Muhammad: You are not alone, Seth! It is a significant issue that several students induce self-inflicted stress by not keeping up with their usernames and passwords to access test results. It's essential to keep track of usernames and passwords to access test scores, as students are responsible for maintaining this information and sending scores with their college applications. School transcripts do not usually contain ACT scores; if they do, they may be outdated. No worries, though. You can reset your account if you remember the email address you used to set up your account. If you have trouble resetting your password, you can use your ACT I.D. number, which is located at the top of your score report from your junior test. If you don't have the score report from a previous test or still need assistance, call ACT at **ACT Customer Care: 319-337-1270**.

Treva: How do I register for the ACT, and how do I register to take the SAT?

Dr. Muhammad: To register for the ACT, go to act.org/bts or actstudent.org and register online. Create an account with the College Board to take the SAT.

Colton: The cost can add up to send my scores to all my schools!

Dr. Muhammad: When registering for the ACT, take advantage of the four free score reports to send to schools. It can be costly to send ACT scores to multiple colleges; it is the student's responsibility.

However, many colleges will allow students to download their scores and send them directly to the college recruiter. Check with the recruiter before paying the high fees that ACT charges.

Jayda: How important are all of these tests, anyway?

Dr. Muhammad: Standardized tests, those seemingly ubiquitous assessments that students encounter on their academic journey, can often be a source of confusion and stress. From the PSAT to the ACT and SAT, these tests significantly affect college admissions and scholarship opportunities. It's important to note that an ACT score of 18 indicates a 50% chance of success at many reputable colleges. Striving for a higher score increases the likelihood of admission and scholarship opportunities. Standardized tests are just one aspect of the college admissions process, and they should be seen as a tool to support and enhance a student's academic aspirations.

While some schools have de-emphasized the role of standardized tests in admissions, it is still wise to approach them with seriousness and preparation. These tests can be valuable tools for students to demonstrate their abilities, even if colleges consider other criteria. Students can open doors to scholarship opportunities and enhance their college application profiles by investing time and effort into test preparation.

.

Popular College and Scholarship Tests

The PSAT: Unveiling Potential and Charting a Course:

Parents say they do not know about the Preliminary Scholastic Aptitude Test (PSAT) each year, and their scholars miss a great opportunity. Although optional and usually not offered to the entire junior or sophomore body, the PSAT is a valuable indicator of a student's academic strengths. It helps them explore potential advanced placement (AP) courses available in the upcoming years. While initially designed for juniors, some schools offer 9th and 10th-grade students the opportunity to take the test. The PSAT may be taken by some students as early as 9th grade, but taking the PSAT as a junior is the only way students can qualify for National Merit Scholarships. Minority students can qualify through a special categorizing.

The scores range from 320 to 1520. Half of the points come from Math, and the other half from the Reading and Writing subtests scored together.

A good PSAT score is above the 75th percentile, but to qualify for National Merit Scholarships, students must score above the 90th percentile.

College Admissions Exams: ACT and SAT

a. ACT: The American Achievement Test The ACT measures a student's achievements in various academic subjects. Colleges and universities widely recognize it as a criterion for admission. While some schools have made these tests optional, many still consider them for scholarship eligibility. Students should aim to score as high as possible on the ACT, which can significantly impact scholarship opportunities.

b. SAT: Scholastic Aptitude Test The SAT evaluates a student's aptitude and potential for college success. It can uncover hidden talents or strengths not reflected in classroom performance alone. The SAT offers a different approach to assessing students' capabilities, showcasing their potential to shine in higher education. While many schools no longer require the SAT, it still holds value in determining scholarship eligibility and should be taken seriously.

Summary of Test-Taking Approaches

a. Take Various Tests: Students may consider taking the ACT and SAT to maximize their opportunities. Each test has its format and emphasis, and a student may perform better on one than the other. If one test does not yield desirable results, the other may showcase their abilities more effectively. Some standardized tests, such as the AP and Junior UCs, cover specific course content, enabling students to demonstrate their knowledge and readiness for advanced coursework.

b. Retaking Tests: If students are dissatisfied with their initial score, they can retake the test. However, preparing adequately and considering the time investment required for further study and practice is essential.

c. Test Security: Students should keep track of their usernames and passwords for accessing test scores, even if the tests are administered at their school. This responsibility helps maintain control over their testing information.

Before the Test Preparation:

1. Start Early: Don't cram. Begin your prep well in advance, ideally several months before the test date.

2. Know the Test Format: Familiarize yourself with the structure and question types on your test.

3. Set Realistic Goals: Determine your target score based on the colleges you're interested in and your strengths and weaknesses.

4. Practice Regularly: Take practice tests under timed conditions to get comfortable with the test format.

5. Study Smart: Focus on your weak areas, but don't neglect your strengths entirely. Balanced preparation is critical.

6. Test-Taking Strategies:

7. Read Instructions Carefully: Don't miss out on easy points due to misinterpreting instructions.

8. Answer Every Question: There's no penalty for guessing, so never leave a question blank.

9. Manage Your Time: Pace yourself. If you're stuck on a question, move on, and return to it later if you have time.

10. Eliminate Wrong Answers: In multiple-choice questions, eliminate incorrect options to increase your chances of selecting the right one.

11. Use Process of Elimination: If you're unsure about an answer, try to eliminate choices you know are incorrect.

Test Day Preparation:

1. Get a Good Night's Sleep: Aim for 7-9 hours of quality sleep the night before the test.

2. Don't Overeat That Morning: Contrary to popular belief, eating can tire students. Fuel your brain the night before with a balanced meal to stay alert during the test. I get it if you are used to eating breakfast in the morning, but be careful not to overeat. Grab an apple, perhaps a kosher granola bar, and juice without sugar.

3.   Arrive Early: Get to the test center with plenty of time to spare so you're not stressed about being late.

4.   Bring the Essentials: Don't forget your admission ticket, valid photo ID, #2 pencils, erasers, and an approved calculator (if allowed).

Mindset Matters:

Stay Positive: Maintain a positive attitude during the test. Don't dwell on difficult questions; focus on the ones you can answer.

For Students Who Don't Test Well

Class Rank/GPA Substitution

Students with high-class ranks and grade point averages can use that merit for automatic admission into some colleges. This is an excellent opportunity for students with low ACT/SAT scores. With Class Rank and GPA substitutions, students may be eligible for the same scholarships at that school as students who submitted test scores. Texas A&M is an example of a school that offers Class Rank/GPA substitution.

Test Flexible Schools

Test-flexible schools are slightly different from regular test-optional colleges. You may submit other test scores instead of SAT/ACT scores at these schools. Acceptable scores will vary depending on the institution. Still, you can generally fulfill the SAT/ACT requirement by submitting scores from AP exams, IB tests, and school-administered placement tests.

Test-flexible schools used to be more common before the pandemic, but now many schools have switched to a test-optional policy. NYU is the only well-known test-flexible school (and they are currently test-optional due to the pandemic).

CHAPTER 17: "MY PARENTS WANT THIS, BUT I WANT THAT."

There comes a time in every lad's life when his desires may be slightly different from his parents' desires for him. It could start with something simple like how his bedroom is kept when he should clean his room...and the student finds himself annoyed at someone who was once viewed as an authority figure not to be questioned. It is not always a matter of who is right or wrong but rather an issue of space, comfort, and independence.

"The Perplexing Parent-Child Dance: Who's Right (Sometimes)?"

The enigmatic world of parents, those peculiar creatures who seem to know everything and nothing simultaneously. We're like a rare Pokémon, complex to understand but undeniably fascinating. So, let's uncover the truth behind the mystical phenomenon of parents being right (almost) all the time!

Now, my dear students, it's time for a reality check. More often than not, parents know what they're talking about. We've been around the block a few (okay, many) times and have amassed a treasure trove of experience. As shepherds over your affairs, imagine we have access to a secret manual to life that we only reveal when a Higher Power permits.

Sometimes, we might be harsh or unfeeling, but parents have the best intentions for their offspring. They genuinely care about your well-being, even if they have trouble expressing it with rainbows and unicorn stickers. Some parents are like walking paradoxes, and the words "I love you" might be their kryptonite, but trust that they care.

Your parents might be the Gandalfs of life, but that doesn't mean you're Frodo, doomed to follow their every word unthinkingly. You're more like Hermione, armed with books and ready to challenge the status quo.

If you ever find yourself disagreeing with your parents, fear not! It's a natural part of growing up. Remember that challenging their wisdom requires a pinch of finesse and a dash of research. Be like Sherlock Holmes, gathering evidence to support your case. Trust us, a well-constructed argument with credible sources will make them pause and ponder.

Now, dear students, let's address the elephant in the room. Yes, there might be a rare, unicorn-like species of rotten parents out there, but rest assured, they're as rare as finding a leprechaun's pot of gold. If your parents are good-hearted individuals who aren't involved in any illegal activities, it's usually wise to trust their guidance.

Remember, trust is a two-way street. Your parents want you to be successful, and while their methods might seem baffling at times, they have your best interests at heart. So, give them a chance, listen to their advice, and try not to roll your eyes too dramatically. It's a delicate dance, my friends, but one worth mastering.

In conclusion, dear students, let's cherish our parents for the gems of wisdom they offer (even if they occasionally seem like the riddlers of our lives). Trust them, as long as they aren't plotting a bank heist, and remember to respect their experiences. But to reiterate, don't forget to embrace your inner Hermione, challenge their ideas with well-researched arguments, and carve your path to success.

Now, go forth, my young adventurers, and navigate the intricate dance between parent and child with grace, humor, and a dash of skepticism. And always remember, every once in a blue moon, you might be the right one!

Disclaimer: This Section is not responsible for excessive eye-rolling or sudden outbreaks of parental-wisdom-induced laughter. Proceed with caution and a sense of humor.

I Want To Be An Astronaut: Anna's Story

I Want to Attend a Four Year College, Mom.

In Ms. Wright's point of view (POV), Anna was an introverted young lady, yet boy-crazy. Ms. Wright secretly feared Anna was naive enough to head for early pregnancy and would undoubtedly be taken advantage of should she attend a university so far from home. In Anna's POV, she felt her mom wanted her to stay home and work in their flower shop. Anna resented her mother for trying to hold her back, yet she had no idea what the actual reason was. Her assumptions about the flower shop were only partially true. However, the lack of communication separated Anna and her mom into tailspins. Given that their relationship had become strained over the college issue, they agreed to discuss it openly.

(Scene: Anna and her mother, Ms. Wright, are sitting at the dining table having a serious conversation.)

Anna: (Excitedly) Mom, I've been thinking a lot about my future after graduation. I want to attend a university instead of going to a two-year college.

Ms. Wright: (Concerned) Anna, I understand your enthusiasm, but attending a university can be expensive. A community college would be a more practical choice. Think about the money we could save!

Anna: I know it's about saving money, Mom, but campus life at a university offers experiences that I don't want to miss out on.

Ms. Wright: (Skeptical) Campus life, huh? Do you mean parties and all that? I worry that you won't take your studies seriously.

Anna: (Defensively) No, it's not just about parties. Let me explain why I want to attend a university.

Ms. Wright: (Skeptical) Go on. But remember, the dishes still need to be washed, and you can't get to our family business late.

Anna: I can explore various majors and courses at a university. I am passionate about art and technology, and many universities offer specialized programs to help me pursue my interests and career goals.

Ms. Wright: Community colleges also have diverse programs, and they offer a strong foundation that you can later transfer to a university, saving you money on general education courses.

Anna: A university will provide me with a more immersive campus experience. I want to live in a dorm, meet new people from diverse backgrounds, and engage in various extracurricular activities, such as joining clubs or volunteering.

Ms. Wright: Community colleges often have a welcoming environment and opportunities for extracurricular involvement, too. You can still meet new people and develop your interests.

Anna: I believe that a competitive university environment will push me to work harder and achieve more. It will challenge me to grow both academically and personally.

Ms. Wright: Community colleges can be just as challenging academically. Besides, it's essential to build a strong foundation before diving into the intensity of a university curriculum.

Anna: Universities often have state-of-the-art facilities and research opportunities that can broaden my knowledge and enhance my skills.

Ms. Wright: Community colleges also offer access to modern facilities and opportunities to engage in research or internships.

Anna: Attending a university will allow me to create a network of contacts and connections with professors and peers that may benefit me in the long run.

Ms. Wright: Community colleges can provide valuable networking opportunities, too. Many students and faculty have connections in various industries.

Anna: (Respectfully) Mom, I understand your perspective, but my heart is set on attending a university. I want to challenge myself and fully immerse myself in the college experience. I want to work part-time or apply for scholarships to help with the costs.

Ms. Wright: (Softening) I appreciate your determination, Anna. I want what's best for you and our family's financial stability. Let's discuss this further and explore all the options together. We can find a balance that considers your dreams and our practical concerns.

Anna: (Smiling) Thank you, Mom. I want to make the most of my college years, and promise I won't take my studies lightly. Let's work together to figure out the best path for me.

Anna's Follow-up Meeting with Dr. Muhammad

Dr. Muhammad: Anna, did you have a chance to speak with your mom about attending a university? (Anna nods). How did it go?

Anna: On the surface, it went well. But I know my mom. Once she decides about something, there's no changing it. She is dead set against me going to Ohio State University.

Dr. Muhammad: Did the two of you come up with a solution?

Anna: Not at all. She stated her opinion, and I said mine. She didn't even tell me why she didn't want me to go to school. She made some excellent points, but she wants me to stay home for personal reasons.

Dr. Muhammad: Personal reasons?

Anna: I work in her flower shop. If I left, she would have to hire someone; she doesn't want to do that.

Dr. Muhammad: I see. Did she tell you that?

Anne: No, but I'm not stupid. The flower shop is our family business. Right now, it's just my mom and me and my siblings. But she wants me to take it over.

Dr. Muhammad: Is that what you want?

Anne: I do, but I want to earn a 4-year degree in business. I feel like I could be more effective.

Dr. Muhammad: The first thing to do is talk with your mom about the flower shop. Give her a chance to explain where and if that fits into her argument about the community college idea. If she confirms your theory, and given that you stated your goal is indeed to take over the flower shop one day, consider engaging in a business project using your Flower Shop.

Anne: What do you mean?

Dr. Muhammad: You stated earlier that your mom wants you to stay home because the business could suffer financially if she has to hire someone.

Anne: Yeah…

Dr. Muhammad: If you initiate and fulfill a small business project, the details could be used to support your scholarship applications. Additionally, your business will benefit. Your business project could involve avenues for students to earn volunteer hours. Your mom could accept student interns and community volunteers. There are so many opportunities that require a business and industry mindset. Another idea you could merge or launch separately would be the web presence of your Flower Business. Is there a streamlined method to take orders online? Could you use the internet to cut down the needed in-person work?

Anne: I like those ideas!

Dr. Muhammad: That's just it. Those are just ideas. You must look at the areas where your business needs support and demonstrate to your mom what a business student can do!

Anne: Well, what is your advice?

Dr. Muhammad: It is a family affair. In your conversation about your reasons for attending a university, the main point that differed significantly from a community college was experiencing college life. It would be best to decide how important that is or any other deal breakers that would prevent you from making the 2-year choice. What is the importance of experiencing campus life for four years instead of the second half of your bachelor's?

On another note, it could be that your business project alleviates some of the financial barriers the business faces. If not, you could consider attending a community college while engaging in business projects and researching locally to aid your business. You could transfer to a 4-year institution in two years and be prepared!

In the end, if you find that attending a 4-year university right off is the best decision, be prepared to take responsibility for some of the drawbacks your mother pointed out. Not that she would say, "I told you so," if the decision turned out to be wrong, and not that you would be sassy enough to disregard your mother's decision with no regard. These things can work better if the decision is joint between the student and their support team.

Dr. Muhammad asked Anna to construct a PowerPoint presentation that detailed her plans. She was asked to include how she intended to pay for college, how she planned to manage to be so far from home, evidence of her chances of success, the financial outlook for her chosen career, the relevance of her career in 5-10 years, and she was asked to list the disadvantages and rebuttal them in the presentation.

Anna took about two weeks to complete the PowerPoint. She presented it to Dr. Muhammad, who poked holes in it, and then Anna had to go back and make revisions, but Anna was super excited about it. Exploring the field of astrophysics taught Anna a lot, and it increased her interest. After fine-tuning her presentation, Anna was ready to defend her position and attempt to convince her mother to support her choice.

Anna: I think I'm ready to talk with my mom now. I can't wait to show her my presentation.

Dr. Muhammad: Building a bridge of understanding takes time and patience. Start by discussing the reasons behind your desire to become an astronaut. Share your enthusiasm, explain the steps you'll take to ensure your safety and emphasize the opportunities for growth and contribution to scientific advancements. Help your mom see that you have carefully considered your path and are committed to making your dreams a reality. If she agrees, present your PowerPoint to her and let the discussion begin after she has seen your entire plan.

Anna: (Sighing) I will try.

Dr. Muhammad: I understand it can be challenging, Anna. However, it's essential to prioritize your happiness and fulfillment. Your dreams matter, and your talent and potential are undeniable. Remember, you have the support and wisdom of your mom, your dad, and the support of the school community, including me, as your college and career counselor. And remember, if your mom is still dead set against it, you still have options. You could consider going to the community college of your mom's choice for two years, and after succeeding there, you could transfer to Ohio State.

Anna: Thank you, Dr. Muhammad. I appreciate your encouragement and guidance. I'll talk with my mom and try to help her see the value and importance of pursuing my dreams.

Dr. Muhammad: That's wonderful to hear, Anna. Remember, you have the strength and determination to overcome any obstacles. I believe in you and your potential to achieve greatness. If you need further support or advice, don't hesitate to reach out. Good luck on your journey to becoming an astronaut!

Anna: Thank you so much, Dr. Muhammad. I feel more confident now. I won't give up on my dreams, and I'll work towards making them a reality.

Dr. Muhammad: That's the spirit, Anna! I'm here to support you every step of the way. Keep believing in yourself, and never stop reaching for the stars. But remember, your mother is your ultimate advocate. You must consider the best plans for you, and with your mother's wisdom, you can become even more successful. She has experience and knowledge about your family dynamics that I do not have. Listen to her with an open mind.

How Baseball Ruled My Family

Early Career Indicators and Presumptions

(Scene: Johnny and his mother, Ms. Price, are in a meeting with Dr. Muhammad.)

Johnny: As a child, I felt the importance of playing baseball because my mom and dad got so excited not only on game days but even going to practice was a huge deal! If my parents argued that morning, a home run from me was the vehicle that calmed the mood. I also learned the value of the sport because my dad could be spotted yelling at the umpire in that scary voice only heard during troubled times. I remember when my dad used his menacing, booming voice for the public to witness. When this argument with the referee took place, it was during one of my best games. There was tremendous positive reinforcement received from my dad later that evening.

I learned to manipulate so well that my balling soon began to drive all family activities—my level of playing determined summer vacations and friendships -my own and my parents' friends. At the end of 6th grade, I determined that no matter what I accomplished, I wanted to play baseball in middle and high school and maybe in college, a place I didn't know much about.

Ms. Price: No, Johnny knew from a young age because his dad and I told him that college is a place he has to go to continue the sports path and also get a good job. The type of college and location were all highly flexible.

Dr. Muhammad: Clearly, baseball was fundamental.

Ms. Price: It wasn't just sports. Johnny was exposed to other opportunities. As a child, he played with building blocks, tinker toys, Mega Cyborg Hand, Picasso Tiles, and other skill-building toys. There was also a good balance between the superhero macho gifts that appealed to him based on the commercials and advertisements. Then, Uncle Frank taught Johnny how to fish, change the oil, and paint the deck.

Dr. Muhammad: All of these activities fall under various potential career clusters. Which of these activities appeal to you the most, Johnny?

Johnny: Baseball. But it doesn't feel the same anymore. I don't necessarily need it in my life.

Ms. Price: Everything changed after his dad and I divorced.

Johnny: Yeah. After my parents divorced, baseball was associated with sadness, arguments, and the disappointment of not making the middle school team.

Dr. Muhammad noted that Johnny picked up engineering skills. Still, his need for family love made him subconsciously choose subjects his unwavering grandfather loved, like fishing courses, Marine Biology, and Advanced Agriscience. Still, the real Johnny was hiding. It would be necessary for Johnny to have conversations and explore his path. Until now, the idea of selecting a career seemed a far-off notion. As a pre-adolescent, it was easy to imagine that things would magically fall into place. Career exploration was needed to clarify what might bring excitement, good wages, and opportunities for advancement.

Dr. Muhammad asked Johnny to consider three future careers he might want to explore. She also assigned him a career interest inventory to complete. They would continue the discussion when it was just the two of them during his upcoming senior appointment.

Follow-up Appointment with Johnny

Dr. Muhammad: Let's discuss the careers you thought about this week. I have the inventory results you shared, but want to hear from you.

Johnny: I've always liked being around sports. One of the happiest times of my life was when I played little-league baseball. I want a job where I can help children develop their gifts.

Dr. Muhammad: Tell me more about how you see your role in helping children.

Johnny: I want to help children who need more than their coaches can give them. You know...the ones who need special attention.

Dr. Muhammad: I heard you say two things that may or may not be related. You said you want to help children who need special attention. You also said you wanted to help with sports-related incidents.

Johnny: Yeah, like a clinic that deals with the total person.

Dr. Muhammad: That sounds exciting--very different from becoming a Marine Biologist. There are so many things you can choose to do! Will you be following your dream to play baseball in college?

Johnny: (Reserved) I would like to pursue baseball if I can, and I would also like to think about some different careers.

Dr. Muhammad: When you took the career interest inventory, it showed you have a propensity toward engineering. Have you attended engineering summer camps to explore those skills and associated careers?

Johnny: No, ma'am. I used to go with my parents every summer to Little League until 6th grade. Besides fishing with my grandpa, I play Fortnite to relax over the summer. I don't feel I know enough about any of the jobs I might like.

Dr. Muhammad: We can look for opportunities for you to explore your career choices more deeply. An internship, a volunteer post, summer camp, or a related job could increase your career exploration.

Johnny: (Getting tired of the discussion) Honestly? I think I will stick with Marine Biology.

Dr. Muhammad: Okay. We have two more minutes. I have one last question, and then we can explore your career options next week. What do you see yourself doing when you get to work every day? Do you go to work, or is your job online? What do you wear to the office? Is it an office? Are you outdoors? Or are you on a ship?

Johnny: (Thinking deeply) I see myself over by the Escambia Riverbank. It is early morning; there is a cool breeze. I'm wearing sweatpants. My grandpa has on his jeans and overalls. We are fishing. I want to work from home.

Dr. Muhammad: I remember your grandfather. He was a Marine Biologist before he retired long ago, right? *(Johnny nods)*. I hope you can share some of your favorite stories about him when we talk next week.

Johnny: My grandfather taught me a lot about fish and different water types…it was pretty cool.

Over the next six months, Johnny attended college and career fairs. He took a few engineering classes, applied to colleges, and completed his FAFSA. He also joined the community baseball team. It was fun, but something was missing. His interest in Marine Biology surfaced higher than his other career choices. However, he explored engineering more seriously as well. Ultimately, Johnny selected a college with strong biomedical engineering and marine biology programs just in case he decided to switch majors.

The quiet shaping from his grandfather had touched his inner heart. Baseball was fun, but not the end all. Johnny knew if he were going to pursue baseball, it should be something he wanted to pursue and not something that would glue his family together.

I'm Scared to Whisper My TRUE Dreams

Dr. Muhammad: Greetings, Arturo. Thank you for completing the Senior Data Collection form. You said you want to major in sociology or become a teacher. Tell me how you decided on that as a major and future career.

Arturo: Hi, Dr. Muhammad. Yes, I've always dreamt of helping families. This is a way I can do that.

Dr. Muhammad: Oh, okay. Helping everyone in the family, or is your focus on a segment of the family like teenagers or elementary students?

Arturo: I want to help the entire family, maybe starting with parents because a lot has to do with assisting Hispanic families with citizenship trouble and working in the United States.

Dr. Muhammad: You sound passionate about this.

Arturo: Well, I'm bilingual, and I already have been helping families by reading and helping to explain how things work in this country for Hispanics and Latinos who want to move here or remain here and work.

Dr. Muhammad: Go on.

Arturo: I've seen a lot of suffering. I was born here, but my parents were not. Some of my family members could not understand anything, which was very frustrating. I had to learn a lot along the way to help everyone.

Dr. Muhammad: I'm impressed with your heart that makes you want to help. With a degree in sociology or teaching, there are different fields you could pursue, depending on in what way you specifically want to help. Perhaps you are considering working in a community center or a government agency. Or do you plan to continue your education and pursue a Master of Social Work? Do you plan to work in a school setting?

Arturo: If I became a middle or high school teacher, I could identify Hispanic students in need. They would have an additional person they could trust, and perhaps they could let me know if they needed immigration help or advice.

Dr. Muhammad: It sounds like two careers if the only reason you would become a school teacher is to identify students whose families need help in areas beyond the classroom. As a social worker, you would need to be sure your work would allow you to focus on a specific population segment.

Arturo: Yeah...to not work with Hispanics and Latinos is a deal breaker. I want to see them through the process of becoming citizens and helping them muddle through legal questions.

Dr. Muhammad: Well, just keeping in alignment with your stated goals, it sounds like you want to help your clients win cases.

Arturo: I do. I want my clients to receive justice. I want to defend Hispanics and Latinos who cannot protect themselves due to not understanding the law and the language barriers. Many of my people are also very poor. All they want is a better way of life.

Dr. Muhammad: Have you thought about immigration law?

Arturo: Well, uh...yes....but...I probably couldn't get that far.

Dr. Muhammad: What am I missing? Your grades are decent. You have passion. Is it what you want to do, or is there something different?

Arturo: No, it's just the thought of me, Arturo, as a lawyer (he laughs). I'm not going to lie. I imagined that, but I would be the first person in my family to go to college, and now, you're talking about me becoming a lawyer?

Dr. Muhammad: Me! (They both laugh). It's my responsibility to encourage you, especially if your past coursework and test scores demonstrate your capacity to succeed at the level of your stated goals. You said you had thought about it.

Arturo: True.

Dr. Muhammad: Clearly, something about being a successful attorney frightens you.

Arturo: I hate to admit it, but you are right. A journey in law is scary. I have never believed in myself like that, though.

Dr. Muhammad: Let's explore your path to becoming an attorney and see if you are up for it!

Come back next week after you have mapped out a plan. I will need you to explain what it would take to become an attorney and if you would be willing to consider it.

I am here to support you if you want to become a social studies teacher, a sociology major, or whatever you decide to pursue, including law.

.

My Mom is Against Me Attending the Same College as my Girlfriend

Darren: Hey, Dr. Muhammad, I've been thinking about my college choices. I want to select my college based on the school my girlfriend will attend. My mom hates her. Truth be told, Agnes, being on campus with me, would be great because she can help me study.

Dr. Muhammad: Ah, I understand you value your relationship, but let's discuss this. Choosing a college based solely on where your girlfriend will go might not be the best approach. It's essential to consider various factors when making such a significant decision. Can I ask you a few questions to explore this further?

Darren: Sure, go ahead. I'm open to hearing your perspective.

Dr. Muhammad: All right, let's start with this. Why do you think your mom is saying selecting a college based on your girlfriend's choice might *not* be the best idea?

Darren: Like I said, my mom hates Agnes. But I want to be close to Anges and maintain our relationship. I think attending the same college would make that easier.

Dr. Muhammad: I understand the desire to be close, but it's crucial to remember that college is a time for personal growth and exploration. It's an opportunity to discover your passions and interests and pursue academic and career goals. Deciding solely based on a relationship might limit your options for self-discovery and independence.

Darren: But we've been together for a long time, and I can't imagine being apart from her.

Dr. Muhammad: I appreciate your bond, but it's also important to recognize that relationships can evolve and change during the college years. College is when individuals experience personal growth and may have different paths to explore. Restricting yourself to a specific college based on a relationship may hinder your ability to fully embrace new experiences and opportunities that could shape your future.

Darren: I never really thought about it that way. But what if we break up while attending the same college? Won't that make things awkward?

Dr. Muhammad: That's a valid concern. Relationships can be unpredictable, especially during the transition to college life. Choosing a college based on a relationship does not guarantee a successful outcome. If a breakup were to happen, it could potentially create unnecessary tension and affect your overall college experience. It's important to prioritize your individual growth and academic journey, ensuring you make the best decision for yourself.

Darren: I see your point. So, what should I consider when making my college choice?

Dr. Muhammad: Great question! When selecting a college, it's important to consider factors such as academic programs, campus culture, personal and professional development opportunities, and the overall fit for your goals and aspirations. Exploring these aspects will allow you to make an informed decision that aligns with your ambitions and interests.

Darren: I guess I need to focus on what's best for my future and trust that our relationship will withstand the distance. It's just hard to let go of the idea of being together all the time.

Dr. Muhammad: It's completely understandable. Relationships require effort and adaptability, especially during significant life transitions like college. Remember, attending different colleges doesn't mean the end of your relationship. It can provide an opportunity for personal growth, independent experiences, and a chance to strengthen your bond by supporting each other's journeys.

Darren: You're right. I need to think long-term and prioritize my education and growth. Thanks for helping me see things from a different perspective, counselor.

Dr. Muhammad: You're welcome! I'm here to support you in making the best decisions for your future. Remember, college is an exciting time to discover new passions, meet new people, and embark on your unique path. Trust yourself and embrace the opportunities that lie ahead.

I'm Taking a Gap Year.

Susan: I'm taking a gap year after high school because I am burnt out. I have no way to pay for college, my grades are not that great, and I also have no idea what I want to be when I grow up, except maybe work as a nurse or run a daycare…but I want to travel first. I never liked school, and that makes it hard.

Enrique: I'm taking a gap year after high school because I was offered the chance to train with Beyonce at a professional dance studio in New York. This is a once-in-a-lifetime opportunity.

Louis: Should I take a gap year? I want to explore my options before committing myself to college for the next four years. I feel like, with my uncertainty, I might just be wasting time. My dad is acting like my life depends on me going straight to college. He never went to college, and neither did my mom. They think I am choosing to fail because I want to wait. True, I was offered a scholarship that will pay for my tuition at Calhoun Community College. As a first-generation college student, I have additional financial opportunities. However, the timing doesn't feel right for me.

Dr. Muhammad: Okay, students, you each have separate scenarios. I will impart general information and hope you can find answers in some of what I say:

Choosing whether to take a gap year after high school is a decision that many students face. A gap year is typically when students take a break from formal education to engage in other activities, such as traveling, working, volunteering, or pursuing personal interests.

Pros of Taking a Gap Year:

Personal Growth and Self-Discovery:

A gap year allows students to explore their interests, passions, and strengths outside the academic environment.

It provides an opportunity for self-reflection, enhancing personal growth, and developing a deeper understanding of oneself.

Expanded Worldview:

Traveling or engaging in cross-cultural experiences during a gap year exposes students to new perspectives, languages, and cultures.

It fosters cultural competence, empathy, and a broader understanding of global issues, preparing students for an increasingly interconnected world.

Clarifying Career Goals:

A gap year allows you to pursue other goals before returning to the formal school structure.

Taking a gap year can help students clarify their career aspirations by exploring different industries or professions through internships, job shadowing, or volunteer work.

It allows students to make informed decisions about their college majors based on real-world experiences.

Development of Life Skills:

During a gap year, students can acquire valuable life skills such as independence, adaptability, problem-solving, and communication.

Engaging in work or volunteer experiences can enhance interpersonal skills, time management, and responsibility.

Renewed Academic Focus:

Some students may feel burnt out after high school; a gap year can provide a much-needed break before pursuing higher education.

Taking time off can reignite students' motivation and enthusiasm for learning, leading to improved academic performance in college.

Cons of Taking a Gap Year:

Academic Disruption:

Delaying college enrollment may result in a temporary loss of academic momentum, making it harder to transition back into a structured learning environment.

It requires careful planning to ensure that the knowledge and skills gained during the gap year align with future academic pursuits.

Financial Considerations:

Taking a gap year may introduce financial challenges, as students often need to support themselves during this period.

The cost of travel, living expenses, and potential loss of potential income may be a barrier for some students.

While colleges will often hold your spot for a year, financial aid is handled differently. Because some scholarships and grants are issued on a first-come, first-served basis, you may have to relinquish those forms of financial assistance and reapply when ready to enroll.

Lack of Structure and Discipline:

Without the structure of formal education, some students may struggle to maintain focus, discipline, and productivity during a gap year.

It requires self-motivation and effective time management to ensure the year is utilized purposefully.

Potential for Detrimental Choices:

During a gap year, students may face distractions or make unwise decisions that hinder their personal and academic progress.

Engaging in negative influences or failing to set clear goals can lead to wasted time and missed opportunities.

The decision to take a gap year instead of immediately enrolling in college is a personal one that should be carefully considered. While a gap year offers unique opportunities for personal growth, self-discovery, and expanded perspectives, it also comes with potential challenges, such as academic disruption and financial considerations. High school students must assess their goals, motivations, and readiness to navigate the pros and cons of a gap year. With proper planning, a gap year can be a transformative and enriching experience contributing to a well-rounded education journey.

I Don't Want to Take Advanced Placement (AP) Classes in My Senior Year

Dear Dr. Muhammad,

I am writing to request a schedule change for the upcoming school year. I know the request is late, but my mom insisted I take all these AP courses for no reason. I fear I will suffer from burnout and not be able to enjoy the best high school year of my life with such a demanding schedule. I am so fed up with people trying to make me do what I don't want to do.

Dear Charlena,

Thank you for your email. Before we discuss your schedule and who will change it if it comes to that, I would like to learn more about what you mean when you say, "I am so fed up with people trying to make me do what I don't want to do." Are we still talking about your schedule? Or is there more? Who is trying to make you do what you don't want to do?

Dear Dr. Muhammad,

No, it is just my schedule. No one is hurting me. I did not mean to come across like that. My issue is specifically with my demanding schedule; my mom and I disagree on what it should be. I am tired of her because she is not the one who will have to be up until 2:00 a.m., sometimes studying for an AP Calculus exam. That's all.

The big decision looming is whether or not to take Advanced Placement (AP) courses in your senior year. I get it; the senior year is often desired as a time to kick back and enjoy less stress. But there are some important pros and cons to consider, especially regarding your college applications.

Pros of Taking AP Courses in Senior Year:

1. College-Ready: AP courses are designed to mimic college-level classes. So, if you can handle them now, you'll be super prepared when you hit campus.
2. Challenge Accepted: They're challenging, so you'll sharpen those critical thinking skills and get used to some academic intensity.
3. College Credit: Many colleges will credit you if you score well on your AP exams. Translation: You could graduate early or explore more electives.

4. Stand Out: Admissions folks love to see students who push themselves academically. Taking AP courses can make you stand out in a competitive college application pool.

5. Subject Love: If you're passionate about a particular subject, an AP course can let you dive deeper into it. Think of it as a gift to your brain.

Cons of Taking AP Courses in Senior Year:

1. Stress Factor: AP courses can be intense. Balancing them with college applications, extracurriculars, and a social life can be like juggling flaming bowling balls. Stress alert!

2. Time Crunch: College applications take time, and AP courses consume a chunk of your schedule. Finding a balance might feel like solving a puzzle.

3. Senioritis Danger: Senioritis is a real thing! Knowing you've already been accepted to college can make staying motivated in those AP classes tough.

4. Burnout Risk: Overloading on APs can lead to burnout. Remember, taking care of your mental and physical health is essential.

Finding the Sweet Spot

So, how do you find that sweet spot between impressing colleges and not stressing yourself to the max? Here's the secret sauce:

1. Be Realistic: Assess your current course load and how much you can handle without becoming a stress ball.

2. Talk to Your Counselor: They're like Yoda for college applications. Chat with them about your goals and get their advice on the correct number of APs.

3. Prioritize: Focus on quality over quantity. It's better to excel in a few AP courses than to spread yourself too thin.

4. Plan Ahead: Think about balancing coursework and college apps. Maybe tackle your more challenging APs in junior year.

5. Self-Care: Remember, it's not just about impressing colleges; it's about your well-being. Don't be afraid to step back if things get too intense.

Ultimately, it's your senior year, and you have the steering wheel. Consider your goals, passion for the subject, and ability to manage the workload. Whether you go full AP or choose a mix of regular and advanced courses, make sure it's a decision that keeps your stress levels in check and your enthusiasm for learning alive and well. You've got this!

Hard Facts About AP Courses

● More than 90% of four-year institutions in the United States grant credit, advanced placement, or both based on qualifying AP exam scores. For more information, visit the following website: www.collegeboard.com/ap/creditpolicy.

● AP course experience favorably impacts 85% of admission decisions of selective colleges and universities.

● AP coursework increases scholarship opportunities and improves chances of college admission.

● The cost of the AP exam is less than most college textbooks.

● Students who take AP courses and exams are much more likely than their peers to complete a college degree on schedule in 4 years. (An additional year can cost your family on average between $18,000 - $29,000). For more information, visit www.collegeboard.com/research

• AP prepares students majoring in engineering, biochemistry, and other STEM (science, technology, engineering, mathematics) majors in college.

• AP students perform better in their intermediate-level STEM coursework than students with the same SAT score who had taken the college's introductory course. Students participating in Advanced Placement are required to take the National AP Exam as part of the courses' curriculum. This testing fee (approx. $95) may be reduced or waived based solely upon the guidelines articulated by the Alabama State Department of Education for free/reduced lunches. Therefore, no student will be denied participation in the AP Program due to financial hardship. It is highly recommended that students consult with the college(s) of choice, as college credit may be earned by scoring a 3, 4, or 5 on the exam. Careful attention should be given when selecting an AP course or courses, as many high schools' schedule-change policies will not allow students to drop an AP course. Consult the grading scale to view the weight given to the rigor of the AP program.

CHAPTER 18: TOOLS AND RESOURCES

College, Scholarships, and Career Planning Tools

ACT - The ACT website provides information on the ACT, including registration, test preparation resources, and score reporting. It also offers career exploration tools and information on college and scholarship opportunities. [Link: https://www.act.org/]

BigFuture - BigFuture, provided by the College Board, offers college search tools, financial aid information, and career planning resources. It also features guidance on preparing for college and succeeding in the application process. [Link: https://bigfuture.collegeboard.org/]

Black College Application – The **Black College Application has roughly 68 member schools** [Link: https://commonblackcollegeapp.com/counselor/]

Cappex - Cappex is a platform that helps students search for colleges, explore scholarship opportunities, and connect with admissions representatives. It also provides tools for estimating college costs and comparing financial aid packages. [Link: https://www.cappex.com/]

Chegg - Chegg is an online platform that offers textbook rentals, study resources, and tutoring services. It also provides college and scholarship search tools and internship and job opportunities. [Link: https://www.chegg.com/]

College Board - The College Board website offers a range of tools and resources for students planning for college. It provides information on college admissions, SAT and ACT preparation, financial aid, scholarship opportunities, and more. [Link: https://www.collegeboard.org/]

College Confidential - College Confidential is an online forum where students can connect with peers, ask questions, and seek advice on college admissions, scholarships, and campus life. It's a valuable resource for gathering insights and experiences from other students. [Link: https://www.collegeconfidential.com/]

College Navigator - College Navigator, a National Center for Education Statistics resource, allows students to search for colleges and universities based on various criteria, such as location, program offerings, and campus size. It provides detailed data on each institution, including graduation rates and financial aid information. [Link: https://nces.ed.gov/collegenavigator/]

College Raptor -College Raptor is an all-comprehensive website that provides college, scholarship, and other financial tools for students, [Link: https://https://www.collegeraptor.com/]

CollegeXpress - CollegeXpress is a website that offers college search tools, scholarship information, and resources for college admissions and test preparation. It also features articles and advice on various aspects of the college experience. [Link: https://www.collegexpress.com/]

College Scorecard - The College Scorecard, provided by the U.S. Department of Education, offers detailed information about colleges and universities, including graduation rates, average costs, and post-graduation earnings. It can help students compare different institutions and make informed decisions. [Link: https://collegescorecard.ed.gov/]

CollegeWeekLive - CollegeWeekLive hosts virtual college fairs and events where students can connect with admissions representatives, explore campuses, and learn about different colleges and universities. It provides a convenient way to gather information and ask questions from the comfort of home. [Link: https://www.collegeweeklive.com/]

CSS Profile-Colleges that use the CSS Profile for financial aid consideration: [Link: https://profile.collegeboard.org/profile/ppi/participatingInstitutions.aspx/]

Fast Facts - Fast Facts, provided by the National Center for Education Statistics, offers quick access to critical data about colleges and universities, including enrollment numbers, tuition costs, and graduation rates. It's a helpful resource for getting a snapshot of various institutions. [Link: https://nces.ed.gov/fastfacts/]

Fastweb - Fastweb is a popular scholarship search engine that connects students with thousands of scholarships based on their interests, academic achievements, and demographic background. It's an excellent resource for finding financial aid opportunities. [Link: https://www.fastweb.com/]

Federal Student Aid - The official website for federal student aid provides information about different types of financial assistance, including grants, loans, and work-study programs. It guides students through completing the Free Application for Federal Student Aid (FAFSA) and helps them understand their financing options. [Link: https://studentaid.gov/]

GoodCall - GoodCall is a scholarship search engine that helps students find available scholarships based on their personal information and interests. It offers a vast database of scholarship opportunities to assist students in funding their education. [Link: https://www.goodcall.com/scholarships/]

Khan Academy - Khan Academy offers free online courses and resources to help students prepare for college entrance exams like the SAT and ACT. It also guides college admissions, financial aid, and college success strategies. [Link: https://www.khanacademy.org/]

My Next Move - My Next Move is an interactive tool provided by the U.S. Department of Labor that helps students explore different careers and find information on job duties, skills required, salary ranges, and more. It can assist students in discovering career options that align with their interests and strengths. [Link: https://www.mynextmove.org/]

Naviance - Naviance is a college and career readiness platform many high schools use. It offers various resources such as career assessments, college search tools, scholarship information, and personalized planning resources to help students navigate their post-secondary options. [Link: https://www.naviance.com/]

Niche - Niche is a website that offers insights and reviews on colleges, K-12 schools, and neighborhoods. Students can use it to research colleges, read student reviews, and explore scholarship opportunities. [Link: https://www.niche.com/]

Occupational Outlook Handbook (OOH) - This comprehensive resource provides detailed information on hundreds of occupations, including job duties, educational requirements, median pay, and job outlook. It can help students explore various career options and make informed decisions about their future. [Link: https://www.bls.gov/ooh/]

Peterson's - Peterson's is a comprehensive resource for college and career information. It offers college search tools, test preparation resources, scholarship databases, and financial aid and admissions guidance. [Link: https://www.petersons.com/]

PSAT- For information about preparing for the PSAT, please read below and visit the following website: http://www.collegeboard.com/student/testing/psat/prep.html.

Roadtrip Nation - Roadtrip Nation is a career exploration platform that offers videos, interviews, and resources to help students discover different career paths and connect their interests with real-world opportunities. [Link: https://roadtripnation.com/]

Scholarship.com - Scholarship.com is a popular search engine that helps students find scholarships based on their profile and qualifications. It provides a wide range of scholarship opportunities from various sources. [Link: https://www.scholarships.com/]

Unigo - Unigo is an online resource that offers college rankings, reviews, and insider information from current students. It also provides scholarship search tools and guidance on college admissions and financial aid. [Link: https://www.unigo.com/]

These resources offer a wealth of information, guidance, and opportunities to support high school students in their post-secondary planning journey. Remember to utilize them wisely, explore the features they provide, and take advantage of the valuable insights they offer. Don't forget to use the resources available at your school's guidance department. They can provide personalized guidance and information about local scholarships, college fairs, and other valuable resources for your school community.

College and Career Interest Inventories

Career interest inventories and career clusters provide valuable insights but are just the tip of the iceberg. Within the **16 main careers Holland describes**, countless lesser-known professions await exploring. Some of these lesser-known careers might offer exciting opportunities and higher pay than the more familiar ones. That's why diving deeper, exploring online resources, seeking internships, and talking to professionals already in the field is crucial. Here are some popular career interest inventories that can assist students in exploring their skills, interests, and values and discovering potential career paths that align with their unique attributes. Students must approach these assessments with an open mind and use the results as a starting point for further exploration and research.

Holland Code Career Test: Based on John Holland's theory, this test assesses individuals' interests and matches them with specific career categories, such as Realistic, Investigative, Artistic, Social, Enterprising, and Conventional. It helps students identify career paths that align with their personality traits. [Link: https://www.truity.com/test/holland-code-career-test]

Substantial Interest Inventory: The Strong Interest Inventory is widely used to assess individuals' interests across various occupational areas. It provides insights into career preferences, work environments, and potential majors or fields of study. [Link: https://www.cpp.com/products/strong/index.aspx]

Myers-Briggs Type Indicator (MBTI): While primarily a personality assessment tool, the MBTI can also offer insights into suitable career paths based on individuals' preferences, strengths, and working styles. It categorizes individuals into 16 personality types. [Link: https://www.myersbriggs.org/my-mbti-personality-type/mbti-basics/]

O*NET Interest Profiler: This online assessment measures individuals' interests in various occupational areas and generates a list of related careers. It provides detailed information about each occupation, including tasks, skills, education requirements, and salary data. [Link: https://www.mynextmove.org/explore/ip]

CareerExplorer: CareerExplorer offers a comprehensive career assessment that explores individuals' interests, personality traits, and values. It provides personalized career recommendations, information on educational requirements, and insights into potential career paths. [Link: https://www.careerexplorer.com/]

VIA Character Strengths: This assessment identifies individuals' core character strengths and virtues. While not explicitly career-oriented, understanding one's strengths can help find careers that align with personal values and motivations. [Link: https://www.viacharacter.org/]

CareerOneStop Skills Matcher: This tool helps students match their skills and abilities with specific occupations. It assesses their proficiency in various skill areas and provides a list of professions that require similar skills. [Link: https://www.careeronestop.org/toolkit/skills/skills-matcher.aspx]

PathSource Career Assessment: PathSource offers a career assessment tool that analyzes individuals' interests, values, personality traits, and skills to provide personalized career recommendations. It also includes information on education and training options. [Link: https://www.pathsource.com/career-assessment]

Sokanu: Sokanu is an online platform offering career assessments based on individual interests, preferences, and skills. It provides comprehensive career profiles, including information on job outlook, salary, and required education. [Link: https://www.sokanu.com/]

Career Key: Career Key offers a range of career assessments that help individuals identify their interests, values, and skills. It provides insights into potential career paths and suggests suitable college majors. [Link: https://www.careerkey.org/]

YouScience - YouScience offers aptitude and interest assessments to help students discover their strengths and explore career pathways. It provides personalized career recommendations based on each student's unique profile. [Link: https://www.youscience.com/]

Careers with Strong Growth Based on Up to a 10-Year Forecast

Here is a list of fields that are projected to have strong growth in the next five to ten years, along with estimated salary ranges:

Aerospace and Aviation:

Aerospace Engineer: Median salary range of $116,500 per year

Air Traffic Controller: Median salary range of $130,420 per year

Aircraft Mechanic: Median salary range of $65,230 per year

Artificial Intelligence and Machine Learning:

Machine Learning Engineer: Median salary range of $112,260 per year

AI Research Scientist: Median salary range of $122,840 per year

Data Engineer: Median salary range of $94,280 per year

Biotechnology and Pharmaceutical:

Biomedical Scientist: Median salary range of $83,600 per year

Pharmaceutical Sales Representative: Median salary range of $73,760 per year

Clinical Research Associate: Median salary range of $65,500 per year

Business and Finance:

Financial Analyst: Median salary range of $83,660 per year

Management Consultant: Median salary range of $87,660 per year

Market Research Analyst: Median salary range of $65,810 per year

Financial Manager: Median salary range of $134,180 per year

Construction and Skilled Trades:

Electrician: Median salary range of $56,180 per year

Plumber: Median salary range of $55,160 per year

Construction Manager: Median salary range of $97,180 per year

Construction Estimator: Median salary range of $65,000 per year

HVAC Technician: Median salary range of $50,590 per year

Creative Arts and Media:

Graphic Designer: Median salary range of $53,380 per year

Film and Video Editor: Median salary range of $63,780 per year

Public Relations Specialist: Median salary range of $62,810 per year

Art Director: Median salary range of $96,650 per year

Multimedia Artist and Animator: Median salary range of $77,700 per year

Public Relations Specialist: Median salary range of $62,810 per year (continued from the previous list)

Culinary Arts and Hospitality:

Chef or Head Cook: Median salary range of $51,530 per year

Event Planner: Median salary range of $51,560 per year

Hotel Manager: Median salary range of $56,690 per year

Education and Teaching:

Elementary School Teacher: Median salary range of $60,660 per year

Special Education Teacher: Median salary range of $61,420 per year

School Counselor: Median salary range of $64,120 per year

College Professor: Median salary range of $80,790 per year

School Principal: Median salary range of $98,490 per year

Engineering:

Civil Engineer: Median salary range of $88,570 per year

Mechanical Engineer: Median salary range of $88,430 per year

Biomedical Engineer: Median salary range of $95,090 per year

Electrical Engineer: Median salary range of $100,830 per year

Chemical Engineer: Median salary range of $108,770 per year

Aerospace Engineering Technician: Median salary range of $67,240 per year

Environmental Science and Conservation:

Environmental Economist: Median salary range of $116,020 per year

Environmental Scientist: Median salary range of $73,230 per year

Conservation Scientist: Median salary range of $63,950 per year

Forester: Median salary range of $63,630 per year

Marine Biologist: Median salary range of $52,470 per year

Park Ranger: Median salary range of $40,240 per year

Wildlife Conservationist: Median salary range of $63,420 per year

Fitness and Wellness:

Personal Trainer: Median salary range of $42,260 per year

Nutritionist/Dietitian: Median salary range of $63,090 per year

Physical Therapist Assistant: Median salary range of $59,770 per year

Healthcare and Medical Services:

Registered Nurse: Median salary range of $75,330 per year

Physician Assistant: Median salary range of $112,260 per year

Physical Therapist: Median salary range of $89,440 per year

Physician: Median salary range of $197,700 per year

Dental Hygienist: Median salary range of $76,220 per year

Occupational Therapist: Median salary range of $86,280 per year

Human Resources Manager: Median salary range of $116,720 per year

Instructional Designer: Median salary range of $66,290 per year

Legal Services:

Lawyer: Median salary range of $126,930 per year

Paralegal: Median salary range of $52,920 per year

Legal Assistant: Median salary range of $52,920 per year

Management Analyst: Median salary range of $87,660 per year

Marketing and Advertising:

Digital Marketing Specialist: Median salary range of $65,810 per year

Market Research Analyst: Median salary range of $65,810 per year (continued from the previous list)

Advertising Manager: Median salary range of $125,510 per year

Mental Health and Social Services:

Mental Health Counselor: Median salary range of $47,660 per year

Social Worker: Median salary range of $51,760 per year

Substance Abuse Counselor: Median salary range of $47,660 per year

Marriage and Family Therapist: Median salary range of $71,340 per year

School Psychologist: Median salary range of $79,820 per year

Nonprofit and Community Development:

Nonprofit Program Coordinator: Median salary range of $50,350 per year

Community Outreach Specialist: Median salary range of $47,160 per year

Volunteer Coordinator: Median salary range of $49,050 per year

Nonprofit and Social Impact:

Nonprofit Program Manager: Median salary range of $70,960 per year

Fundraising Manager: Median salary range of $120,690 per year

Social Entrepreneur: Salaries vary widely depending on the venture and funding.

Renewable Energy and Sustainability:

Solar Photovoltaic Installer: Median salary range of $46,470 per year

Wind Turbine Technician: Median salary range of $56,230 per year

Environmental Engineer: Median salary range of $94,220 per year

Green Building Architect: Median salary range of $81,440 per year

Solar Energy Systems Engineer: Median salary range of $96,270 per year

Environmental Scientist and Specialist: Median salary range of $73,230 per year

Energy Engineer: Median salary range of $85,880 per year

Sustainability Manager: Median salary range of $116,910 per year

Technology and Information Technology (IT):

Software Developer: Median salary range of $110,140 per year

Data Scientist: Median salary range of $98,230 per year

Cybersecurity Analyst: Median salary range of $103,590 per year

Cloud Architect: Median salary range of $131,200 per year

UX Designer: Median salary range of $77,200 per year

IT Project Manager: Median salary range of $88,240 per year

Transportation and Logistics:

Supply Chain Analyst: Median salary range of $68,730 per year

Logistics Coordinator: Median salary range of $48,780 per year

Transportation Manager: Median salary range of $97,630 per year

Truck Driver: Median salary range of $47,130 per year

Welder: Median salary range of $45,190 per year

These approximate salary ranges vary based on experience, location, and industry. It's also important to consider other factors like job satisfaction, work-life balance, and personal interests when choosing a career path.

Twenty of the Highest-paid Medical Doctors Fields

The field of medicine offers various specialties, each with its earning potential. While neurosurgeons are often among the highest-paid medical professionals, other areas also command high salaries. Here is a list of 20 of the highest-paid medical doctor fields and their areas of expertise:

Orthopedic Surgeon: $533,872 to $734,098 per year

Plastic Surgeon: $400,000 to $700,000 per year

Cardiologist: $423,000 to $589,000 per year

Gastroenterologist: $380,000 to $576,000 per year

Radiologist: $415,000 to $589,000 per year

Anesthesiologist: $362,000 to $462,000 per year

Dermatologist: $385,000 to $550,000 per year

Ophthalmologist: $330,000 to $518,000 per year

Urologist: $339,000 to $500,000 per year

Otolaryngologist (ENT): $365,000 to $500,000 per year

Radiation Oncologist: $386,000 to $487,000 per year

Neurologist: $280,000 to $407,000 per year

Neurosurgeon: $616,901 to $776,464 per year

Cardiothoracic Surgeon: $438,000 to $613,000 per year

Pediatrician: $181,000 to $278,000 per year

Endocrinologist: $197,000 to $310,000 per year

Hematologist/Oncologist: $305,000 to $438,000 per year

Psychiatrist: $220,000 to $320,000 per year

Rheumatologist: $222,000 to $342,000 per year

General Surgeon: $298,000 to $471,000 per year

Job Descriptions for Twenty of the Highest-paid Medical Doctor Fields

Orthopedic Surgeon: Specializes in the musculoskeletal system and performs surgeries related to bones, joints, ligaments, and tendons.

Orthopedic Surgeon: $533,872 to $734,098 per year

Plastic Surgeon: Focuses on reconstructive and aesthetic surgeries to enhance appearance and repair physical defects.

Cardiologist: Specializes in diagnosing and treating heart-related conditions and diseases.

Gastroenterologist: Deals with the digestive system and its disorders, including the esophagus, stomach, liver, and intestines.

Radiologist: Utilizes medical imaging technologies to diagnose and treat diseases and injuries.

Anesthesiologist: Administers anesthesia and monitors patients' vital signs during surgeries or medical procedures.

Dermatologist: Diagnoses and treats conditions related to the skin, hair, and nails, including skin cancer.

Ophthalmologist: Specializes in eye care, including diagnosing, treating eye diseases, and performing eye surgeries.

Urologist: Focuses on the urinary tract and the male reproductive system, treating conditions such as kidney stones and prostate issues.

Otolaryngologist (ENT): Deals with the ears, nose, and throat, including hearing and balance disorders, sinus conditions, and throat infections.

Radiation Oncologist: Specializes in treating cancer patients using radiation therapy.

Neurologist: Diagnoses and treats disorders of the nervous system, such as epilepsy, stroke, and Parkinson's disease.

Neurosurgeon: Performs surgical interventions on the brain, spinal cord, and nervous system.

Cardiothoracic Surgeon: Performs surgeries on the heart, lungs, and other organs in the chest cavity.

Pediatrician: Provides medical care for infants, children, and adolescents, focusing on their physical and mental well-being.

Endocrinologist: Deals with hormonal disorders, including diabetes, thyroid conditions, and reproductive system issues.

Hematologist/Oncologist: Specializes in diagnosing and treating blood disorders and cancers.

Psychiatrist: Focuses on diagnosing and treating mental health disorders and prescribing medications when necessary.

Rheumatologist: Treats autoimmune and musculoskeletal disorders, such as arthritis and lupus.

General Surgeon: Performs various surgical procedures across different medical specialties.

These approximate figures can vary based on experience, geographic location, work setting, and additional factors like bonuses and benefits. It's essential to consider multiple sources and conduct further research for more precise and up-to-date salary information.

Seven Types of Engineers and What They Do

Aerospace Engineer:

Aerospace engineers design, develop, and test aircraft, spacecraft, and related systems.

They work in industries like aerospace manufacturing, defense, and space exploration.

Responsibilities include aerodynamics analysis, structural design, propulsion systems, navigation and control systems, and air and space travel safety.

Biomedical Engineer:

Biomedical engineers apply engineering principles to healthcare and medical research, often working at the intersection of biology, medicine, and technology.

They develop medical devices, equipment, and technologies, such as prosthetics, medical imaging systems, and diagnostic tools.

Tasks involve designing and testing medical equipment, collaborating with medical professionals, and contributing to advancements in healthcare technology.

Chemical Engineer:

Chemical engineers design and oversee processes for producing, transforming, and utilizing chemicals and materials.

They work in pharmaceuticals, chemicals, energy, food processing, and materials science industries.

Tasks may include designing chemical processes, optimizing production, developing new materials, and ensuring safety and environmental compliance.

Civil Engineer:

Civil engineers plan, design, and supervise the construction and maintenance of infrastructure projects and systems essential to modern life.

They work on projects like buildings, bridges, roads, water supply systems, wastewater treatment plants, and environmental protection.

Tasks involve designing structures, analyzing soil conditions, managing construction projects, and ensuring compliance with regulations.

Electrical Engineer:

Electrical engineers design, develop, and maintain electrical systems and components, from power generation and distribution to electronic devices.

They work in electronics, telecommunications, power systems, and automation.

Responsibilities include circuit design, troubleshooting electrical systems, developing control systems, and ensuring safety and compliance.

Mechanical Engineer:

Mechanical engineers design and develop mechanical systems and devices that range from small components to large machines.

They work in the manufacturing, automotive, aerospace, energy, and robotics industries.

Responsibilities include designing machinery, conducting simulations, testing prototypes, and improving the efficiency of mechanical systems.

Software Engineer/Developer:

Software engineers develop, test, and maintain software applications, systems, and platforms.

They work in various domains, including web development, mobile app development, game development, and software for embedded systems.

Tasks involve coding, debugging, software architecture design, collaborating with cross-functional teams, and staying updated on programming languages and tools.

Remember that these descriptions provide a general overview, and engineers' specific tasks and projects can vary widely based on their specialization, industry, and individual roles. Many engineers collaborate with professionals from other disciplines to create innovative solutions to complex problems.

Engineer Salaries and Future Outlook

Software Engineer/Developer:

Potential Earnings: Software engineers are among the highest-paid engineers. Earnings can vary widely based on experience, location, and specialization. In the US, entry-level software engineers may earn around $70,000 to $100,000 annually, while experienced professionals earn over $150,000 annually.

Future Outlook: The demand for software engineers continues to be strong, with increasing reliance on software and technology across industries. The job market is expected to remain favorable, with artificial intelligence, cybersecurity, and mobile app development opportunities.

Mechanical Engineer:

Potential Earnings: Mechanical engineers earn a median annual wage of around $88,430 in the US. Earnings can vary based on industry and specialization.

Future Outlook: Mechanical engineering is diverse, and job prospects are generally stable. Advances in renewable energy, automation, and sustainable manufacturing could offer new opportunities for mechanical engineers.

Electrical Engineer:

Potential Earnings: Electrical engineers earn a median annual wage of around $100,830 in the US. Earnings can vary based on experience and industry.

Future Outlook: With the continued growth of electronics, automation, and renewable energy, electrical engineers are expected to have solid job prospects. Emerging technologies like 5G, electric vehicles, and intelligent grids may drive demand.

Civil Engineer:

Potential Earnings: Civil engineers earn a median annual wage of around $87,060 in the US.

Earnings can vary based on specialization and location.

Future Outlook: Civil engineering is tied to infrastructure development and maintenance. The demand for modernizing and creating sustainable infrastructure and urbanization should provide opportunities for civil engineers.

Chemical Engineer:

Potential Earnings: Chemical engineers earn a median annual wage of around $108,770 in the US. Earnings can vary based on industry and experience.

Future Outlook: Chemical engineers play a role in pharmaceuticals, materials, and energy industries. Advances in biotechnology, renewable energy, and sustainable manufacturing could drive demand for their expertise.

Biomedical Engineer:

Potential Earnings: Biomedical engineers earn a median annual wage of around $95,090 in the US. Earnings can vary based on specialization and location.

Future Outlook: Biomedical engineering is expected to see growth as healthcare technology advances. Opportunities may arise in medical device development, tissue engineering, and healthcare informatics.

Aerospace Engineer:

Potential Earnings: Aerospace engineers earn a median annual wage of around $116,500 in the US. Earnings can vary based on specialization and experience.

Future Outlook: Aerospace engineers work on aircraft, spacecraft, and related systems. With the growing interest in space exploration, commercial aviation, and defense, the demand for aerospace engineers could remain strong.

It's important to note that technological advancements, economic conditions, and global trends can influence the future outlook for any field. The COVID-19 pandemic and other unforeseen events can also impact job markets and industries. To stay informed about the most up-to-date information, it's advisable to consult recent sources such as government labor reports and industry publications.

Calculating Your Unweighted and Weighted GPA

Calculating your unweighted GPA is relatively straightforward, as it's based solely on your grades without any extra weight for honors or AP courses. Here's a step-by-step guide on how to calculate your unweighted GPA:

Step 1: Gather your grades.

Collect your final grades for all your classes. Typically, these grades are given on a 4.0 scale, with A being 4.0, B being 3.0, C being 2.0, D being 1.0, and F being 0.0.

Step 2: Assign a numerical value to each grade.

Convert your letter grades to their corresponding numerical values. For example:

A = 4.0

B = 3.0

C = 2.0

D = 1.0

F = 0.0

Step 3: Calculate your GPA.

Add up all the numerical values of your grades.

Divide the total by the number of classes you've taken.

Here's the formula: GPA = (Sum of Numerical Grades) / (Number of Classes)

For example, if you've taken five classes and your grades are as follows:

A (4.0)

B (3.0)

A (4.0)

C (2.0)

B (3.0)

Your unweighted GPA would be calculated as follows: GPA = (4.0 + 3.0 + 4.0 + 2.0 + 3.0) / 5 = 16.0 / 5 = 3.2

So, your unweighted GPA in this example would be 3.2.

GPA Calculators:

Many online GPA calculators are available to help you calculate both your weighted and unweighted GPAs. These calculators typically allow you to input your course grades and credits, and they'll provide you with the GPA based on the information you provide. Some popular GPA calculators include:

College Board GPA Calculator: The College Board provides a free GPA calculator that allows you to input your grades, course credits, and course levels (such as honors or AP) to calculate both weighted and unweighted GPAs.

Naviance GPA Calculator: If your school uses Naviance, they often provide a GPA calculator that you can access through your Naviance account.

Online GPA Calculators: Many websites and apps offer GPA calculators, such as GPACalculator.net, GPAcalculator.io, and more. Search for "GPA calculator" in your preferred search engine or app store.

These calculators can help you quickly determine your GPA, making it easier to track your academic progress.

The Common Application - What You Need to Know

Using the Common Application can save students time and effort when applying to college. The platform simplifies the process of submitting applications to multiple colleges and provides a standardized format for colleges to review applications. However, it's important to note that not all colleges accept the Common App, and some schools have their own application systems. Therefore, students should carefully research the application requirements for each college they plan to apply to. Some Common App member institutions prefer that students apply directly with them, not via the Common App. It's also worth noting that some college recruiters have mentioned that they cannot access student applications when they apply through the Common App.

Here are some key features and components of the Common Application:

1. Online Application Form: The Common App provides a standardized online application form that allows students to input their personal information, academic history, extracurricular activities, and essay responses.

2. Application Essays: Students can write and submit their personal statements and supplemental essays through the Common App. Many colleges require these essays as part of the application.

3. Recommendation Letters: The Common App facilitates the submission of recommendation letters. Students can request letters from teachers and other individuals, and these recommendations are sent directly to the colleges.

4. Academic Transcript and Test Scores: Students can input their academic records, and some institutions allow you to self-report test scores (e.g., SAT or ACT).

5. Application Fees: Students can pay application fees through the Common App, and some colleges offer fee waivers for eligible students.

6. College List: You can select the colleges you want to apply to from a list of institutions that accept the Common App. It's a time-saving feature for students applying to multiple schools.

7. Supplemental Materials: Some colleges may require additional materials, such as portfolios for art programs or resumes for specific majors. The Common App helps manage these materials.

8. Application Deadlines: The platform allows you to see application deadlines for each college and track your progress in completing applications.

9. Application Fee Waivers: You can apply through the Common App if you qualify for fee waivers based on your financial situation.

10. Mobile Application: The Common App offers a mobile app, making it easier for students to work on their applications from their smartphones.

ABOUT THE AUTHOR

Dr. Dedra Lori Muhammad

Author Dr. Dedra Muhammad is an independent education and writing consultant. She served as a public school educator and college counselor for over two decades. Earlier in her career, she served as a counselor for students in grades K-8 in Indiana and Georgia.

Her curriculum vitae includes producing programs to help diverse groups of seniors from rural, low-income, and urban areas raise millions of dollars in scholarships every year. Dr. Muhammad has been immersed amidst the behaviors of more than 250,000 students during her career. She is steeped in knowledge of trends in education, system barriers, and struggles some teenagers endure when it comes to making the most out of high school. She has worked as an administrator in a homeless facility; she has done extensive work in domestic violence awareness and prevention. The musicals and stage plays Dr. Muhammad produced have themes permeating cultural diversity, education, abuse prevention, predatory lending --and other issues plaguing families and societies.

Dr. Muhammad has worked with artists and groups such as WHODINI and Chuck D. from Public Enemy #1 to bring awareness to challenging problems like gun violence, date rape, land grabs, and crimes against the elderly.

She is the mother of twins Shafi and Hanif, and a widow after being married to Phillip Muhammad, her beloved husband, for 25 years. Dr. Muhammad is a graduate of the University of Michigan in Ann Arbor, Indiana University (IPFW), and Capella University.

Dr. Muhammad is also the organizer of the Rising South Literacy School. Dr. Muhammad has been referred to as an "Artistic Genius" and as "The Good Doctor." Her 5-star novel, "Hidden Princess: The Rebirth of Making Mary," is the first in an underway trilogy.

For more information, go to www.dedramuhammad.com.

BOOKS BY THIS AUTHOR

Hidden Princess: The Rebirth Of Making Mary

Hidden Princess is breathtaking, historically accurate, and the most compelling love story imaginable. In a triangular love affair, one man refuses to stop until he is granted access into the forbidden chambers of the princess. Yet, another man posing as her knight has swallowed the key to keep her safe and pure until their pending nuptials. Set mostly during the transition between the Civil War and the Great Depression, Hidden Princess chronicles the daily travails of a nation – and its people– in flux. The Johnson family soon succumbs to the lure of the Great Migration, joining millions of other poor Black families who are seeking the gifts promised to them under the spell of the North Star.

Black Male Resilience Following Homicide In Predominantly Black Neighborhoods: A Qualitative Study

The public health concern about gun violence in urban neighborhoods prompted the research question, "What is the resilience experience of men in the Black community following the homicide of a male resident of a predominantly Black neighborhood in their city?" Whether homicide is initiated by other Black men or by law enforcement lethal intervention, community survivors experience perceived vulnerability, fear, community trauma, and stigma that places undue stress and pressure on the greater community members who may not have personally known the victim. Studies on the impact of normalized devaluing Black life and intergenerational consequences for the greater community are limited, which means the process of communities moving past the consequences represents a gap in the literature. The basic or generic qualitative research methodology used in this project required semi-structured interviews to capture the study participants' attitudes and opinions and answer the research question.